# CONTENTS

# FOREWORD

## PETER MARCUSE

Fifty years ago, people such as the authors of the chapters in this book—researchers, social advocates, and people concerned with inequality in housing and its effects—drew maps very much like the striking one in Tom Angotti's introduction, showing the dramatic range and spatial concentration of inequalities in the city. But the figures they used were not about race, ethnicity, or color, but physical condition. Those were indeed correlated with physical conditions, as they are now, but the indicators of inequality were measured by the presence or absence of running hot and cold water, rooms per person, plumbing facilities, and quality of maintenance. They measured what the census termed "substandard" conditions of the housing unit. A critical review of the situation then summarized it as holding:

> Good housing is standard housing: waterproof, having adequate plumbing, not falling down. With less than x persons per room (or y, depending on their sex). A suitable neighborhood is simply a neighborhood of good housing; so no problem there (Marcuse 1971).

The key indicator of social conditions, if they were considered at all, was often held to be the rent-income ratio, or, more questionably, the home ownership rate. The key housing policies about which controversies erupted were rent control, and building code standards and enforcement.

This book reflects a considerably changed view of things. Spatial location, and spatial concentration of housing, by categories of race and ethnicity, with emphasis on the closely related pricing of housing and its financialization, have come to take a prominent place in housing policy debates. The relevant policies continue to include rent regulation, now more modestly called rent stabilization rather than rent control, and zoning policies that directly address questions of location and neighborhood composition. These have become more and more important in establishing what we would consider "good housing."[1] This book puts these latter considerations front and center.

Further changed are not only the emphasis on the spatial aspects of race and ethnicity, but the policy approaches to dealing with race. Fifty years ago, the socially repugnant treatment of members of minority groups was addressed primarily by laws against discrimination, the passage of anti-discrimination legislation, fair housing acts. But it is not so easy to prove discriminatory intent in cases involving clearly disparate racial results from housing actions, particularly given the present composition of the Supreme Court.

The problem is simple: a racially disparate—negative—result can be brought about without ever mentioning race. Because of major disparities in incomes and wealth and political power between blacks and whites, the market will itself automatically have a discriminatory effect, grouping lower-paid black workers differently into separate locations from their more prosperous white fellows. It doesn't require an intent to discriminate, even if it could be shown in judicially cognizable fashion, to produce a discriminatory spatial result; the market will do it all by itself.

The tools of planning have not adapted well to this changed manifestation of the problem. Talking explicitly about race is still a no-no to a confused or ill-willed majority of the Supreme Court. Explicitly racial-based zoning categories will not pass judicial muster today. Yet that would be a frontal way to attack the underlying problem, which is indeed one that comes with the historical connection between race and income. This book suggests what is in a way a path around this problem: community-based planning, specifically resulting in zoning that is justified not because it affirmatively treats racially defined groups fairly, but because the communities want it. Zoning is being explored as a concrete way of implementing a truly fair and just distribution of housing and space in the city.

That raises a further issue, one playing a minor role 50 years ago, but in the forefront of controversial planning issues today: the issue of displacement. Insecurity of occupancy was always a major concern in housing, but focused on economic factors: inequality of incomes leading to inequalities in the availability of housing on the market, a shortage of affordable housing, with rent controls and public housing as the progressive answers then. Neither is adequate today, and the cases in this book highlight the issue. Rent controls have their limits, not only in terms of political feasibility but also because rising costs require rising rents to break even, and rent regulations take that into account. Public housing faces similar political problems, and even when it is provided does not deal with its spatial consequences; tenants of public housing are overwhelmingly minorities these days. The typical public housing project in New York City today, apart from elderly housing, is less than 10 percent white.

Today's insecurity of occupancy is only secondarily like the risk of eviction for inability to pay the rent of the old times. Its cause is quite different.

It has nothing to do with increases in the operating costs of housing, or the greed of landlords benefiting from a shortage of housing units in the city. It comes rather from a changing pattern of land prices, a major component of the costs of housing, both rental and owner-occupied. In a way, it has less to do today with the poverty of the 99 percent than with the wealth and preferences of the 1 percent. The homeless are still with us, and poorly treated both by the city's government and by the private market, but not in ways that influence the demand of the 1 percent. Their demand is rather for locations that are spatially desirable and already occupied, but by those of much lower income. The result is the process now called gentrification, which results in the displacement of lower class residents by higher income people, with the resulting widespread insecurity that characterizes much of affordable housing today. Poverty is not the cause of displacement; wealth is. Which is, incidentally, why a focus on reducing inequality is today much more important than a focus on reducing poverty, which is only one component of inequality.

Again, zoning looms large among the tools of planning that is at the center of conflicts involving inequality in housing, and specifically inequality in spatial benefits; and again, the cases in this book suggest community-based planning as one of the appealing mechanisms to deal with the problem. Good zoning can help, but bad zoning can do great harm. To be equitable, zoning must be part of a comprehensive and democratic planning process, one which takes into account not only individual neighborhoods but also the fair distribution of the benefits of living in the city to all of its residents, not only to those who already have them or can buy them for themselves at the expense of others.

The following chapters lay out the roots of the problem and describe in concrete detail the way they are working themselves out in three lively, detailed case studies, and end with a proposal of what can be done to remedy the situation. It's a challenging presentation, highlighting the difficulties as well as the potentials, the forces for change and equality as well as the forces for preservation and extension of an unjust status quo. Hopefully, the book will help bend the arc of planning at least a bit more towards justice.

**Endnotes**

1. Just what "good housing" might mean, in terms of successful "multi-cultural integration," beyond spatial integration, remains an inadequately explored issue, but material for another book.

# PREFACE TO THE 2023 EDITION

## TOM ANGOTTI AND SYLVIA MORSE

New York City is, as it has been throughout its history, brutally unequal. Wealth hoarded in sky-high empty penthouses is protected by police violently removing unhoused people from the streets and subways. City plans, budgets, and elections are made undemocratically. But New Yorkers, as throughout the city's history, continue to fight for racial and economic justice, particularly through the struggle over land.

When we set out to write *Zoned Out!* in 2016, New York City was experiencing major demographic shifts with an influx of white people and their wealth citywide and in neighborhoods of color, resulting in displacement of poor and middle-income people of color. At the same time, the city had undergone another transformation: massive neighborhood rezonings first undertaken under New York's billionaire mayor, Michael Bloomberg, covering nearly 40 percent of the city's land area and slated to continue under its new mayor, Bill de Blasio. This policy of widespread but ad hoc neighborhood rezonings drove many New Yorkers not only to learn about zoning and the city's planning processes, but to try to understand the connections between these zoning changes and the displacement they were seeing and experiencing—and to fight them. The growth of grassroots organizing around zoning can be seen in the case studies in this book; the 2003 Frederick Douglass Boulevard Rezoning in Harlem saw very little engagement, but by 2008 neighborhood residents were well-organized in opposition to the 125th Street Rezoning.

As expressed in our original introduction, *Zoned Out!* was a work of advocacy planning, written to capture this particular era of planning and housing policy that was dominated by neighborhood rezonings and inform community organizing and expertise.

Today, racial segregation and displacement persist citywide and at the neighborhood level. White people make up about 30 percent of the population citywide, but nearly half in Manhattan and less than 9 percent in the Bronx. Black New Yorkers continue to be priced out, bought out, and evicted. From 2010 to 2020, the citywide population grew by 7.7 percent while the Black population declined by 4.5 percent—mostly in Brooklyn.[1] Black and Latinx tenants are more likely to be severely rent-burdened and to live with worse housing conditions than white renters.[2] Finding and holding onto housing at all is a challenge. Less than a quarter of New Yorkers have incomes high enough to afford the average apartment available for rent. Finding an apartment for less than $1,500 per month is nearly impossible, as less than 1 percent are vacant[3] and newly built housing is more expensive.[4] Landlords and New York's housing courts evict thousands of people from their homes each year. As a result, homelessness has reached record highs, with more than 100,000 New Yorkers having slept in city shelters in 2022 and thousands more on the street, the vast majority of whom are people of color.[5] These housing challenges are compounded by the larger crises including the COVID pandemic, climate collapse, and rising white supremacist organizing and ideology.

While the problems of social inequality in New York remain familiar, there have been important changes in the housing, planning, and organizing landscape which should be taken into consideration while reading this book.

## RACIAL JUSTICE AND ANTI-DISPLACEMENT ORGANIZING INFLUENCES CITY ZONING POLICY

Anti-displacement and racial justice organizing had a significant impact on zoning policy throughout the de Blasio mayoralty and it continues today under Mayor Eric Adams.

Bill de Blasio became mayor in 2013 on a platform decrying the growing economic and social divide between rich and poor communities that Bloomberg had only expanded. His Mandatory Inclusionary Housing (MIH) Program, enacted in early 2016, required that developments in rezoned areas include a percentage of income-restricted and permanently rent-stabilized housing. MIH was a response to community organizing against Bloomberg-era rezonings and housing inequality—but it also became a target. Grassroots anti-displacement groups and housing nonprofits alike protested MIH over concerns that the percentage of regulated apartments was too low and that they would not target low-income people at greatest risk for displacement. De Blasio's plan for MIH was tied to 15 proposed rezonings, mostly in low-income neighborhoods of color that had been passed over in Bloomberg's rezoning blitz. While the administration argued that it selected these neighborhoods as part of a strategy to address housing inequality, it was also responding to the availability of cheap land and enormous pools of global and local capital looking for new places to build outside of the city's developed core—Bloomberg's adored "luxury city."

Local and citywide organizing against neighborhood rezonings led to several of the proposed plans being dropped, and to an array of policy and funding commitments as part of the approved plans.[6] Toward the end of de Blasio's tenure, city planning prioritized rezonings in two areas that were predominantly white and higher-income, the SoHo/NoHo and Gowanus rezonings.[7] This change in strategy was another case of a simultaneous testament to and a target of anti-displacement organizers, who opposed the inadequate low-income housing and potential to increase speculation pressures on nearby lower-cost housing.[8]

Communities also successfully resisted several big development plans in low-income neighborhoods of color, including the Amazon headquarters in Queens and the Industry City rezoning in Sunset Park. Abolitionists fighting a plan to build four new jails, purportedly as part of a (nonbinding) plan to close the Rikers Island jail complex, collaborated with anti-displacement activists who shared their knowledge of the land use review process. Though the plans were approved, the campaign commanded responses from public officials and, moreover, represented the anti-racist principles and solidarity across movements that had come to define much of the land use activism in the city. Years of anti-displacement organizing also led to the passage of a law in 2021 requiring Racial Impact Studies as part of rezonings, a small step forward but still a signal that the discourse on racial impacts of zoning policy has changed.

It is now rare to see city planners characterize zoning plans as "race neutral," a once-common refrain described in this book.

This doesn't mean that city planning policy is now anti-racist. The Bloomberg-era rhetoric of "increasing the tax base" and attracting Richard Florida's "creative class" (Florida 2017) may have been replaced by citations of Richard Rothstein (Rothstein 2017) and condemnations of exclusionary zoning, but the policy prescription remains largely the same: design zoning policy around real estate industry demand, without meaningful investment in low-income housing. Long-dominant arguments that housing costs are solely a product of supply and demand, which ignore the complexity of housing submarkets and the racial impacts of capital investment in historically redlined neighborhoods, are being repackaged with the rhetoric of social justice by advocacy groups under the branding of YIMBYism (as in, Yes in My Backyard). The plan for SoHo/NoHo, for instance, which allowed for more, mostly non-rent-regulated housing to be built in one of real estate's most sought-after neighborhoods, was backed by YIMBY groups as simultaneously a strategy to prevent wealthier people from gentrifying lower-income neighborhoods of color *and* as a way to integrate the neighborhood. While MIH does offer stronger affordability measures in these neighborhood rezonings, subsidy levels and rent regulations are nowhere near the level of need and the ripple effect of rent and land value increases on adjacent low-income communities of color is still downplayed.

Zoning changes without sufficient public investment will not help house poor people, and certainly do not challenge the racist and undemocratic control of land. As much as this book explores the power of zoning to deepen inequities, it shows its limitations as a housing policy tool. While upzoning can increase land values and exacerbate displacement pressures, so can downzoning (as shown in the Harlem and Chinatown case study chapters, in particular). Zoning regulates how big a building can be and what kinds of things it can be used for, which is too blunt and inadequate a tool to address the complex social and economic factors that affect housing affordability—let alone tenant power.

With this understanding, housing movement groups have seen renewed focus and significant wins on housing policies and models beyond the realm of zoning that are making inroads against displacement and housing inequality.

## ANTI-DISPLACEMENT MOVEMENTS BUILD TENANT POWER AND FIGHT AUSTERITY

After years spent largely resisting rollbacks to renters' rights, tenant organizers have gone on the offensive. In 2019, statewide tenant organizing led to the Housing Stability and Tenant Protection Act (HSTPA), which addressed loopholes that had weakened rent stabilization. HSTPA has prevented rent hikes that would have financially and socially destabilized tenants and legally destabilized thousands of apartments.[9] It has also changed the equation for speculators who previously overpaid for rent stabilized buildings with business plans dependent on evicting tenants and deregulating rents. Challenges remain: in 2022, the Adams administration's Rent Guidelines Board approved the highest rent increases since Bloomberg, and landlord lobby groups are pushing to repeal components of the HSTPA. Tenant organizers continue to work on strengthening rent stabilization and expanding protections for currently unregulated tenants through proposed Good Cause Eviction law.

Across the housing movement, people are resisting evictions. In 2017, following years of advocacy, New York City established the Right to Counsel in housing court, which has helped tenants remain in their homes.[10] Tenant union and eviction defense organizing has also grown, particularly during the COVID pandemic. In 2020, nonprofit reformers and grassroots groups coalesced under the banner of #CancelRent, helping to win life-saving eviction moratoriums and rent relief funding from the State. Since evictions have resumed, reformers have continued their work to expand and adequately fund the Right to Counsel, while grassroots tenant groups organize eviction blockades and build tenant unions.

New York City also has a growing movement to consolidate and fortify the cornerstones of movements for housing in the public domain, a concept we cite in *Zoned Out*. It is sometimes referred to as "social housing," including cooperatives, public housing, and other models that take land and housing out of the private market so that it may be stewarded for the public interest. The city has seen particularly powerful growth among the movement for Community Land Trusts (CLTs), one such model of community-controlled land and housing. The CLT movement has been led by unhoused New Yorkers and tenants with a particular focus on racial justice and a reparative approach to land ownership and community wealth-building. Since *Zoned Out!* was first published in 2016, at least twenty new CLTs are in development across the five boroughs with new public funding. CLTs and allies are advocating for laws and funding at the city and state level to expand tenant-controlled land and housing and address the underlying problems of land commodification. CLTs can be vehicles for political education and community organizing, strengthening communities' power to respond to city plans, and providing a model for democratic, community-based planning.

At the same time that the concept of social housing is garnering new champions, however, public housing continues to be defunded and threatened by policies that privatize or weaken public housing programs. In order not to replicate the shift from public and low-income housing to middle-income, public-private "affordable housing" models seen in the latter half of the twentieth century (discussed in Chapter 2), the movement will need to define its terms on anti-racism, democratic tenant control, and housing for those who need it most while rejecting neoliberal concepts of "self-sustainability."

Finally, a burgeoning focus of the housing movement is on addressing the root problem of austerity politics. Housing groups continue to address unfair tax incentives like the expired 421-a program which provided tax exemptions to developers while reducing city tax revenues and failing to serve low-income tenants. They are also looking at other aspects of tax policy, including addressing inequities in New York State's property tax system that benefit homeowners and burden tenants and to establish a tax on house-flipping. Unhoused and tenant organizers are paying particular attention to funding for low-income housing, including expanding voucher programs and investing in housing over shelters. The uprisings against racism and the police state in 2014–2015 and 2020 built momentum around demands to divest from policing and invest in services of care, including housing.[11] In sum, much of the progress on housing policy has emerged through and been strengthened by solidarity across movements for racial justice, labor, migrant justice, and abolition of the Prison Industrial Complex.

**WHAT'S NEXT?**
Amidst housing movement successes, communities continue to face undemocratic development and zoning plans that threaten to increase displacement pressures.

Mayor Eric Adams' planning and housing agenda, while it has not yet focused on neighborhood rezonings, includes a range of citywide initiatives aimed at increasing housing production through big real estate's forever wish list: zoning deregulation, less public review, and more tax breaks. For instance, the administration's zoning proposals would help convert office buildings and hotels emptied by the pandemic into housing. This will only help landowners and investors maximize rents and miss an historic opportunity to create low-income housing unless adequate subsidies and regulations are provided. Albany is taking a similar approach. At the time of this writing, Governor Kathy Hochul proposed state mandates for housing production that would drive zoning and housing changes across local jurisdictions statewide and each Community Board in New York City. While this approach takes some important steps to address exclusionary zoning in towns and suburbs across the state, it does not include regulations against rent gouging or true investment in low-income housing in the public domain.

A newly-elected New York City Council, which includes many younger, first-time elected officials (some who come out of leftist and progressive organizing), is still finding its footing in how to challenge Mayor Adams' austerity budgets and create land use policy beyond the focus on developer-initiated and neighborhood rezonings. The body needs to overcome its dependence on the system vesting enormous powers in the mayor and the siloed city agencies that the office controls.

The city still has never produced a comprehensive plan, which could be developed through a combination of community-based and citywide planning to equitably distribute resources. The fight to increase democracy in planning continues, from organizing anti-racist political education at the building and neighborhood level to fighting for public involvement in the development and approval of plans.

Above all, as emphasized throughout this book, communities and activist planners must continue to fight against zoning without planning. Displacement is one spatial expression of racial capitalism, of wealth inequality enforced through labor exploitation and land-hoarding. The city's housing and racial justice movements show us the solutions are in building systems that strengthen worker and tenant power and that share and protect land resources through collective ownership and democracy.

We are all still learning what planning for an equitable and just city looks like. The answers will be found with the New Yorkers fighting for racial and economic justice and the right to the city.

Note: The case studies have been reproduced as in the original 2016 version and have not been updated. The editors are confident that their analyses remain valid.

#### Endnotes

1. Population, Change Over Time (2010 to 2020), U.S. Decennial Census (Department of City Planning, New York City Population FactFinder); New York City Department of City Planning Population Division, "Dynamics of Racial/Hispanic Composition in NYC Neighborhoods: 2010 to 2020," November 10, 2021.

2. New York City Department of Housing Preservation and Development, "2021 New York City Housing and Vacancy Survey Selected Initial Findings," May 16, 2022 ("NYC HVS").

3. NYC HVS, 2021.

4. A portion of newly constructed income-restricted housing is offered at rents of $1,500 or below, but not the majority, and not nearly enough to meet the scale of need. (*Reviewing The Mayor's Housing Plan to Bolster Affordability and Equity*, New York City, Public Advocate Jumaane D. Williams, December 2021; Sam Stein, Community Service Society of New York, *Assessing De Blasio's Housing Legacy*, February 2021; New York City Independent Budget Office, *Affordable for Whom? Comparing Affordability Levels of the Mayor's Housing New York Plan With Neighborhood Incomes*, February 2019).

5. Coalition for the Homeless, 2022 Fact Sheet.

6. The first neighborhoods where rezonings were proposed and approved included East New York, Brooklyn, Jerome Avenue in the Bronx, Bay Street, Staten Island, Inwood and East Harlem in upper Manhattan, and Far Rockaway and the Flushing Waterfront in Queens. Other neighborhoods including Bushwick, Brooklyn and Southern Boulevard in the Bronx were eyed but not ultimately rezoned during de Blasio's tenure.

7. Notably, these were not historically white, low-density neighborhoods like those in Staten Island, the North Bronx, South Brooklyn, or parts of Queens. Both were former industrial neighborhoods that had been gentrifying since the 1980s. About a quarter of Gowanus's population is Black or Latino, albeit declining, and largely concentrated in the neighborhood's public housing.

8. In addition to tenants and organizers concerned about racial justice and displacement, some opponents were white homeowners in these areas and other advocates more focused on historic preservation, construction and shadow impacts, and other issues not related to housing affordability.

9. NYC HVS 2021 Selected Initial Findings.

10. Prior to the passage of the Right to Counsel law, just 1% of tenants in New York City facing an eviction in housing court had a lawyer. Since the law passed, as much as 71% of tenants had legal representation during a given quarter, and the vast majority were able to remain in their homes. (Office of Civil Justice, 2021).

11. In 2016, the Movement for Black Lives' "Vision for Black Lives" Policy Platform demanded "investments in Black communities, determined by Black communities, and divestment from exploitative forces including prisons, fossil fuels, police, surveillance and exploitative corporations" at the local and federal levels. In 2020, calls to Defund the Police nationally included unprecedented mobilization around New York City's budget with demands to cut the NYPD budget by $1B, and resulted in modest (mostly cosmetic) reallocations of funds that year. Since then, local organizations focused on policing and carceral systems continue to organize for "budget justice," drawing attention to disparities in spending on police and jails over housing, education, and social services.

# ACKNOWLEDGMENTS

This new edition of *Zoned Out! Race, Displacement and City Planning in New York City* is dedicated to the memory of **Michael Sorkin**, the founder and moving force behind UR Books, publisher of the original edition of this book. Michael headed the **Terreform** urban design studio and the Urban Design degree program at City College of New York. He dedicated his life's work to advancing progressive and revolutionary approaches to cities and their great human potential. Sadly, he was an early casualty in the COVID pandemic.

When Tom first approached Michael with the idea for this book which would include contributions by activists and professionals engaged in the struggles against rezonings in working class communities of color, Michael didn't miss a beat and said "Yes, let's do it." Michael's response was indicative of his enduring commitment to social justice in his professional practice, his pedagogy, his writings, and timely works that were released by **UR Books**, which was a project of Terreform. Michael aimed at provoking discussion and debate about social justice issues around the world, issues that were usually relegated to footnotes in mainstream publishing. To name just a couple, *Gowntown: A 197-x Plan for Upper Manhattan* poked holes in the city's faux community planning by putting forth bold ideas that were never considered by the city, and *Waterproofing New York* saw beyond the city's half measures dealing with storm surges and sea level rise while challenging everyone to think bigger and more creatively. Another of Michael's platforms was the Institute for Urban Design in New York City which he led.

Michael loved New York City, and his vision for better urban futures extended far beyond New York. He prepared a bold plan for the City of Jerusalem that would have been jointly managed by Palestinians and Jews. Through UR books he tackled other controversial international issues. We urge all readers to check out the rich offerings from UR Books (www.urpub .org/books).

Much of Michael's work at Terreform was made possible by professionals like **Cecilia Fagel**, who was the moving force behind UR Books operations. Cecilia worked closely with the co-editors and book designer **Isaac Gertman** on many details in the text and layout of *Zoned Out!*. She engineered the marketing and distribution as well.

We would also like to recognize the passing of another great urbanist, **Peter Marcuse**, who wrote the foreword to *Zoned Out!* and contributed much to our discussions on displacement. He was part of our group of activists and scholars who met regularly to consider filing a lawsuit against New York City's zoning practices for violation of the national fair housing law. We dropped that idea but moved quickly to shape this publication that would uncover the key issues we had discussed.

Throughout the world, Peter was known as a leading scholar in the fields of housing, urbanism and planning. His list of publications and awards is impressive but less well known is his lifelong commitment to progressive and radical urban theory and practice. Peter bridged the gap between theory and practice. At the peak of Civil Rights activism, he was part of progressive organizations such as *Planners for Equal Opportunity* and its successor *Planners Network (PN)*. He was a regular contributor to the *PN Newsletter*, *Progressive Planning Magazine,* and *Progressive City*.

When Peter chaired the urban planning program at Columbia University in the 1970s he organized a conference that boosted proposals for radical reform of the New York City Charter allowing for community control while challenging the mainstream proposals that would stifle the voices from the grassroots and civil rights movements. He was also part of the Right to the City Coalition and supported initiatives for housing Justice led by Picture the Homeless. Peter was a prominent advocate for tenant rights and rent regulation and a central figure in the rise of the citywide movement promoting community land trusts. He was also an outspoken critic of the policies guiding the rebuilding of Manhattan after 9/11 which fueled luxury development and turned its back on communities of color.

This work benefited from engagement with community organizers, residents, and business people who have been confronted with the official narrative on development and zoning and refuse to accept it. Their ideas have helped to shape the arguments advanced here. We hope to have injected some of the passion and love for their communities that they have demonstrated in their daily practice. Among the many we could acknowledge, we note the contributions of activists **Nellie Bailey, Alicia Boyd**, and **Andrew Padilla** to the struggles against displacement.

We are especially grateful for the support and cooperation of **Joan Copjec**, Michael Sorkin's widow and Terreform board member, who generously gave New Village Press the opportunity to publish this revised edition.

# INTRODUCTION

**TOM ANGOTTI**

From afar, New York City seems to be a global model of multicultural integration. Visitors and residents see a wonderful rainbow of ethnicities and colors on the streets, in the subways, and neighborhoods. Some parts of the Borough of Queens have pockets of residents from every country in Asia and Latin America. Parts of Brooklyn are home to Afro-Caribbeans, Africans, African Americans, and Latinos. While many have left for the suburbs, there are still significant pockets of European immigrant groups—Irish, Italians, and Polish, for example. This looks a lot like the wonderful rainbow that former Mayor David Dinkins, the city's first African American mayor, once posited as an ideal.

This image of New York City as a haven for immigrants from all over the world is embedded in its history. In 1855 Walt Whitman, in *Leaves of Grass,* proclaimed, "Here is not merely a nation but a teeming nation of nations." The city projects the image of ethnic tolerance, the beacon of hope for all humanity symbolized in the Statue of Liberty. Most recently, the city's leaders have branded it the "capital of the world," open for business to all who arrive.

But the reality for most New Yorkers has always been more complicated. This city, once a major center for the slave trade, has a long history of ethnic and class conflict. Throughout its history, most newcomers wound up living in segregated enclaves instead of being assimilated into the mythical "melting pot."

Today, New York City is one of the most segregated and unequal cities in the world. The island of Manhattan, at its center, the ultimate (and only) destination for many outside visitors, is the most unequal of all counties in the nation (Roberts 2014). Beyond Wall Street, Times Square, and the luxury towers and town houses lie the apartment blocks, row houses, and public housing where working people live. The divide between Wall Street (the 1 percent) and the 99 percent is gaping; the luxury condos selling for up to $100 million are not far from the 59,000 homeless people sleeping in shelters every night; and the billion-dollar bank headquarters hover above

# 00.A Black-White Segregation in New York City

One dot= 200 people

■ Black

▓ White

U.S. Census Bureau, American Community Survey, 2014 5-year Estimates.

the huge pool of service workers in bars and restaurants making sub-standard wages without any benefits.

The inequalities do not stop at Manhattan's borders. The rest of the City of New York has three times as many residents as Manhattan (over six million compared to two million), and the differences in wealth and living conditions between Manhattan and the rest of the city are obvious to anyone who ventures off the island of skyscrapers. The inequalities continue throughout the metropolitan region, which has two and half times the population of the core city and the greatest household income gap among all metropolitan areas in the nation.[1]

One of the most striking examples of New York City's segregation is the geographic divide between black and white people. This follows a long history of racial separation and oppression, starting with slavery, extending through the Civil Rights Movement and today's struggles for justice in the face of police violence. As shown in Figure 00.A, blacks and whites in New York City live separately today, almost 50 years since the Fair Housing Act prohibited discrimination in housing.

Racial separation by itself might not be a problem, but it correlates with and reinforces unequal access to quality schools, healthy food, safe streets, and overall quality of life. And yet, another expression of the structural inequalities in New York City is the threat of displacement constantly facing low-income residents and people of color.

In one of the most dynamic land markets in the world, increasing home prices and rents constantly churn over neighborhoods. These changes often benefit property owners, but renters—the majority of New Yorkers—are constantly on the run, forced to pay higher rents and priced out. Entire neighborhoods are transformed by gentrification, which may bring certain improvements to the neighborhood but results in the displacement of the most vulnerable, particularly low-income people of color. Indeed, displacement, and not just rising rents and prices, has historically been one of the greatest threats to African American, Latino, and other minority communities, and the struggles against displacement have been an integral part of the civil rights and social justice movements (Hartman et al 1981; Angotti 2008).

This is the context for this study and narrative. The purpose here is not to describe the inequalities or to paint a detailed picture of the city and its region. Many others have done this quite well (Caro 1975; Fitch 1993; Mollenkopf and Castells 1992; Sites 2003). The purpose is to throw some light on how it got that way, and how the city's planning and housing policies have contributed to and helped create this condition. This will disprove the myth that displacement follows some mysterious natural law that cannot and should not be challenged. We will end with some proposals for changing the way the city relates to its neighborhoods and addresses questions of racial and economic inequality.

The immediate impetus for this study comes from the intense struggles of the last decade by neighborhood activists across the city to cope with massive new development pressures. As we write, the city is in the midst of several intense zoning battles. These follow the massive rezonings that took place under the administration of Mayor Michael Bloomberg (2002–2014), which have abetted new development and transformed the face of many older neighborhoods into playgrounds for high-stakes real estate investment. The rezonings were instrumental in the Bloomberg strategy to promote the luxury city and attract both capital and the people that have lots of it (Brash 2011).

A unique aspect of the rezoning proposals under the present mayor, Bill de Blasio, is that they are located largely in communities of color—African American, Latino, and Asian. In response to outcries from these neighborhoods, the city administration has promised to work with the neighborhoods, address their issues, and provide more opportunities for affordable housing. Mayor de Blasio, who took office in 2014, brandishes his plan to create 200,000 new units of affordable housing. De Blasio ran on a platform that highlighted inequalities, a sharp contrast with his predecessor, Michael Bloomberg, and the previous mayor, Rudolph Giuliani, who famously alienated large sectors of the African American and Latino communities.

This study will demonstrate that there is much more continuity with past policies than most supporters of this administration will admit. Indeed, Mayor de Blasio's approach to planning and housing follows the long tradition of government acquiescence to the carving up of the city into separate enclaves for rich and poor, for black, white, and brown people, creating many other mini enclaves.

This book is a work of advocacy that we undertook in order to contribute in a timely way to the heated debate over zoning, affordable housing, gentrification, and displacement in New York City. It relies on scholarly work in the field, but most of all it benefits from the collective intelligence and experience of the activists who have been fighting to protect and improve their neighborhoods, and professionals who have worked with them. It also relies on observations by professionals from their own practice. For this reason, some things are argued without reference to outside

**4**

sources. We stand by these arguments and invite readers to analyze and criticize the analysis on its merits.

# LOCATION, LOCATION, LOCATION

The driving force behind all of this is the real estate market, which seeks new opportunities for investment in favorable locations that yield the highest economic return (the ABC's of real estate are commonly known as: location, location, location). Higher returns on investment in land mean higher rents and home prices. Since these rising housing costs are not matched by increases in income levels for working people, new development means more displacement and segregation—unless government steps in to balance the scales.

This is the proverbial real estate capital of the world, and when prime locations are ripe for development, the real estate industry presses city government to provide the appropriate set of planning and housing policies that will help them realize the future value of their investments in land. It is no coincidence that the single largest contributor to the campaigns of local elected officials is the real estate industry.

The city's planning and housing bureaucracies are responsible for translating the needs of the real estate industry into policy. They appear at community meetings to advise people that development is coming and declare that the only thing anyone can do is to adapt and perhaps get some small benefits out of it. Market-rate development and rezoning are presented as some mysterious forces that cannot be stopped. The city uses its authority to create an air of inevitability that robs people of any power to control the future of their communities. The city's planning department promotes exercises in community-based planning, but whenever neighborhoods have developed their own well-reasoned plans the official planners throw them away. This happens even after the City Planning Commission has officially reviewed and approved the community plans, as the chapter on Williamsburg shows.

While real estate is charting the direction of land use policy, this is usually not obvious. Nor is it clear that the elected and appointed officials who introduce and vote for changes in land use policy understand the long-term consequences of their actions or even bother to understand them. However, our purpose here is not to assign blame, but to reveal how real estate and the public sector work together; not to rectify the inequalities created by the real estate market, but to evade responsibility for them.

We aim to show how together they fuel displacement and create instability in communities of color while protecting more affluent white enclaves. In unison with the significant opposition to these changes, we claim that displacement matters because it has disrupted the lives of entire populations in the United States that have historically been forced to move when they do not want to, starting with Native Americans and African Americans (Fullilove 2016). We are not simply a multi-ethnic city; we are a city of displaced and segregated people.

# RACE MATTERS

Thus one of the central themes in this study is that race matters. Displacement negatively affects communities of color while white communities, beneficiaries of white privilege, tend to be either protected or have access to comparable or better living conditions elsewhere.

It is impossible to fully understand the city's development history without tracing the ways that race has always mattered. This is especially timely because one of the most important struggles in the city today is captured in the phrase, "Black Lives Matter," a sound rebuke to the broken windows policing that claims racial neutrality. We will show that planning and housing policies, like policing, are not "race neutral" or "color blind," contrary to what may be the best intentions of some of the city's policymakers. Indeed, when making planning and zoning policy, there is little or no deliberation about displacement and its effects on communities of color, much less any serious, concrete measure to address it.

We are far from being a color-blind city or society. The remarkable racial and cultural diversity we witness in our daily tapestries bides a hopeful future. However, in planning as with policing, race matters.

# ORGANIZATION OF THE BOOK

In Chapter One we offer a brief primer on the city's land use and zoning policies and the ways that displacement and race intersect with them. We then briefly trace the long history of racialized land use and housing policies in Chapter Two, a reminder that the problem has deep roots that will require substantial efforts to undo. Then we offer three recent case studies that illustrate how rezonings have resulted in the displacement of communities of color—in Williamsburg (Brooklyn), Harlem, and Chinatown (Manhattan). Our final chapter offers alternatives to the status quo—community-based planning and direct public investment in housing that remains in the public domain, starting with the New York City Housing Authority.

These and many other alternatives can only work, however, if there is a fundamental shift in the way the city does planning. The Department of City Planning must drop its exclusive reliance on zoning and engage in true long-range planning as a collaborative effort with the residents and businesses in its diverse neighborhoods, ever conscious of the social, economic, and environmental impacts of its policies and practices. We need planning that is both top-down and bottom-up. And once we rid ourselves of the myth that zoning will solve the city's housing problems, it will be possible to rescue and add to the significant stock of existing affordable housing by using public resources more effectively, without attaching them to the private development machine.

**Endnotes**

1. "Income Inequality Data for Metro Areas," *Governing*, accessed January 5, 2016, http://www.governing.com/gov-data/economy-finance/Metro-Area-Gini-Index-Map.html.

# CHAPTER ONE

# LAND USE AND ZONING MATTER

**TOM ANGOTTI**

This chapter looks at how land use and zoning actually function in New York City. It is not a primer, though we do offer the readers a thumbnail sketch of the basics. Rather, it is an analysis of how land use and zoning are driven by powerful political and economic forces, principally the real estate industry.

New York City has never adopted a master plan—a long-term comprehensive plan for the utilization of land. It is the only major city in the United States that has never charted a strategy that would help shape the city's future. Using federal funds, the Department of City Planning completed a master plan in 1969, but it was opposed by the real estate industry and never seriously discussed or approved by the City Planning Commission.[1] Comprehensive planning looks at the future, projecting trends and integrating all aspects of urban life while outlining policies to guide decision-making by government. The city's powerful financial and real estate industries appear to be quite satisfied without it.

# WHAT IS ZONING?

New York City doesn't do comprehensive planning, but it does zoning. The main instrument for land use planning and regulation is the Zoning Resolution. The Zoning Resolution broadly controls:

- How land may be used (either for residential, commercial, or industrial purposes, or a combination of these);[2]
- How much can be built on the land (mainly through a formula that sets a maximum Floor Area Ratio [FAR]—the built floor area divided by the total land area); and
- How much land must remain unbuilt.

The Zoning Resolution includes the *Zoning Text*, which defines permitted uses, maximum building sizes, and open space requirements, and *Zoning Maps*, which indicate where that text is to be applied. The first Zoning Resolution was established in 1916; it was rewritten in 1961 and is constantly changing as the result of revisions to the text and the maps.[3]

While zoning in New York City is complex and highly technical, it is also very political. Since the Zoning Resolution is so big and intricate, it can give the appearance that zoning is not political and strictly the purview of independent technocrats whose only commitment is to further "the public interest." It follows, then, that lay persons in neighborhoods who raise questions or objections to zoning proposals are often branded as parochial, uninformed, emotional, racially biased, and if opposing a rezoning that

**10**

would spur new development, driven by exclusionary "Not in My Backyard" sentiments. The zoning experts, however, though they may think and act in accordance with the very same sentiments, tend to be immune to any challenge. Since zoning remains mostly under the control of the experts, and since the use of land is regulated mostly by zoning, there is a serious deficit of open, democratic discussion and debate about the things that really matter to New Yorkers and how they can participate constructively in charting the future of the city.

Zoning remains under the control of the experts, and since the use of land is regulated mostly by zoning, there is a serious deficit of open, democratic discussion and debate about...the future of the city.

## THE CITY PLANNING COMMISSION AND DEPARTMENT OF CITY PLANNING

The City Planning Commission (CPC) is a 13-person body that votes on zoning changes. The majority of appointments (seven) are made by the Mayor, who effectively controls the body, though it was created as a semi-independent body. Each of the five borough presidents appoints a commissioner and the Public Advocate appoints one.

The Department of City Planning (DCP) is the line agency made up of career professionals and employees. DCP's director is also chair of the CPC, and appoints an executive director. The Mayor has effective control of agency policy through his/her appointees, and it is a well-established practice for there to be extensive communication between City Hall and the agency. Both are sensitive to the largest elephant in the room—the real estate industry, which relies on zoning as a predictable regulatory tool that can be flexible enough so that it changes to meet the needs of the real estate market. Developers understand zoning as the machine that must function well in order to meet the needs for growth and development while protecting the most valued real estate. While some developers may grumble about the time and cost involved in dealing with zoning, the larger and more experienced ones understand that it's better to have a predictable regulatory environment and pay established legal and lobbying firms to make sure their needs are met.

# HOW IT REALLY WORKS

So much for the basics. This was not intended as a manual to teach people all they need to know about zoning, so there are many details and complexities that we will not cover. For detailed information, readers may consult the DCP website, where they will find the *New York City Zoning Handbook* and other information.[4] What follows is our understanding, based on our experience, of how zoning actually works, including both the formal, official process, and things that occur outside of it. It is an interpretation; the planners in DCP, developers and others who have a direct stake in the process will have other interpretations. The following shows how the zoning machine works, and doesn't work, in our neighborhoods and is intended to throw light on what seems from the outside to be a highly technical arena, but in practice is deeply entwined with the real estate market. We will deal with upzoning, downzoning, contextual zoning, and hybrid rezonings, and explain how DCP thinks about the zoning process.[5]

*Upzonings* are proposed wherever DCP determines that there is significant development potential. An upzoning generally increases the amount of square feet of building that can be developed. This is important for property owners, especially developers, for whom the time and effort involved in a zoning change has a payoff. The planners survey all blocks in the area with an eye to determining which lots are either vacant or not built out to their maximum potential under existing zoning. These are called "soft sites" or "underutilized" parcels of land. When there is significant excess floor area available for building, a lot appears to be ripe for development. The planners may conclude that a zoning change is needed to provide a greater incentive to spur development by the market. In a hot real estate market, one-story commercial buildings, auto-related uses, and small residential buildings are often targeted as "underutilized," an assessment that mirrors the views and interests of landowners, investors, and speculators who are anxious to develop the properties and would love to maximize the returns on their investments by increasing allowable densities.

## 01.A Upzoning on Fourth Avenue in Brooklyn.

*The 2003 Park Slope Rezoning increased the residential density of Fourth Avenue, which had traditionally served as a commercial corridor with low- to mid-rise housing, while maintaining the low-rise character of adjacent side streets.*

**Prior to Rezoning**

R6
FAR .78–2.43
Building Height
Max 65'
Typical height
prior to rezoning
30'–40'

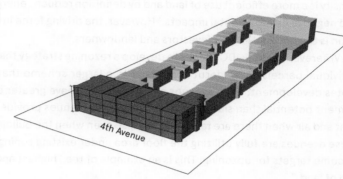

**After Rezoning**

R8A
FAR 6.02
Building Height
Max 120'
Base Height
Min 60'
Max 85'

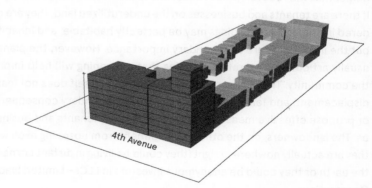

It is important to understand that for planners and developers it is the land that is "underutilized," even when people are living or working there; developers make good money when the underutilized land they own is upzoned, increasing its value exponentially. This is what is known as the principle of "highest and best use"; if the market dictates a more intensive use and the zoning does not permit it, then the planners should amend the zoning to allow for this development. The planners may justify this by reference to environmental and planning logic—for example, that higher density is a more efficient use of land and by definition reduces energy use and negative environmental impacts.[6] However, the driving force in operation is the bottom-line for investors and landowners.

Wherever possible, DCP seeks to develop a rezoning strategy that links individual parcels of "underutilized" land to a larger scheme that promotes development. Wide avenues are presumed to have greater development potential than side streets because wide avenues provide more light and air when there are taller buildings; so even when the buildings on these avenues are fully utilizing the floor area under existing zoning, they become targets for upzoning. This is an example of the "highest and best use of land."

The designation of underutilized land functions very much the way the term "slum" was used decades ago to target communities of color for demolition and redevelopment under the federal urban renewal program. If there are tenants and businesses on the underutilized land, they are rendered invisible; their buildings may be perfectly habitable, and inhabited, but the inhabitants are of secondary importance. However, the planners usually articulate a narrative claiming that a rezoning will help improve the community. They often claim that upzoning by itself does not lead to displacement, and fail to seriously analyze the secondary consequences or propose effective measures to protect existing tenants and businesses. The landowners, on the other hand, benefit from upzoning even when they are actually nowhere in sight (they could be living in distant corners of the earth or they could be anonymous investors in LLCs—Limited Liability Corporations).

A change in zoning from a manufacturing district to residential or mixed-use usually functions as an upzoning because it expands development potential. Mixed-use districts permit both residential and industrial uses, but since rents for residential uses are much higher than for industrial, mixed-use districts are likely to become residential when the area is experiencing new growth. This is what happened with the Williamsburg and Greenpoint rezonings starting in 2005, which resulted

**14**

in the deindustrialization of these traditionally mixed residential-indus-trial neighborhoods. The mixed-use zoning had the effect of *eliminating* mixed uses. City Planning's deceptively named mixed-use districts were introduced in a way that seemed to placate the strong desire among resi-dents and businesses to preserve the historic mixed-use character of the neighborhood (see Chapter Three).

One dramatic recent example of an upzoning is Fourth Avenue in Brooklyn, approved over a decade ago. This major thoroughfare borders the Park Slope neighborhood, a notable brownstone district, which for the most part has benefited from zoning protections. Before it was upzoned, Fourth Avenue was home for many low- to mid-rise apartment buildings and small business-es with a largely Latino population. The upzoning resulted in the displacement of residents and businesses and the construction of high-rise luxury towers and upscale businesses.

Downzoning involves a reduction in buildable floor area. This may occur in places where communities strongly oppose new development and want to minimize chances that underutilized sites will be built on. DCP often seeks to balance a downzoning with an upzoning in the same area. If there is little de-veloper interest in an area and local elected officials are strongly behind it, the planners may be more receptive to calls for downzoning. Downzoning often takes the form of contextual zones.

*Contextual zones* were introduced in the 1980s in response to criticisms that the city's zoning rules were based on the tower-in-the-park model, which allowed tall buildings and required open space at the ground level—the typical "Manhattan model." This kind of development faced mounting oppo-sition when pressures outside Manhattan started producing towers in low- to mid-rise row house neighborhoods, many of them middle- and upper-in-come homeowners, many of them white. Contextual zoning restricted new development so that the built form would look more like existing development in a given neighborhood.

Contextual zones are designed to maintain existing neighborhood scale and character in residential zones. They have been used extensively in places such as Brownstone Brooklyn, where they limited building heights at the street wall, building fronts had to line up, and front yard parking was prohibited. For exam-ple, much of Park Slope in Brooklyn is protected by contextual zoning (in addi-tion to restrictions on redevelopment placed by the Landmarks Preservation Commission). See the map above showing both the Fourth Avenue rezoning area and Park Slope's contextual zones. (See Figure 01.A)

Contextual zoning has been perceived as a popular preservation tool. DCP's 2015 citywide proposal, "Zoning for Quality and Affordability," would stretch the building envelope in contextual zones; it faced opposition by many neighborhoods and preservation groups who have generally supported contextual zoning.

Contextual zoning and downzoning began in and are predominant in white, middle-income, homeowner neighborhoods. Without any public discussion of the racial and income disparities apparent since its introduction, contextual zoning has thrived. It is now proposed throughout the city—including some communities of color—as a means of convincing reluctant communities that new development won't overpower the existing built environment.

*Hybrid* rezonings involve both upzonings and downzonings in the same neighborhood. Wherever possible, DCP seeks to balance upzoning and downzoning, often including contextual zones in the mix. Hybrid rezonings appear to balance preservation and new development, and therefore help promote the image that the city planners are independent technical people who are not predisposed to either of these options, but committed to finding harmony between them. In some ways, all rezonings are to one degree or another hybrid rezonings. Hybrid rezonings, many of them in gentrifying neighborhoods, follow several rationales:

- **Wide avenues vs. side streets.** Wide avenues are upzoned and a adjacent side streets are downzoned and/or contextually zoned. The assumption is that there is much greater potential for high-rise development on wide avenues, and when the side streets are protected this helps alleviate fears of adjacent residents, particularly homeowners. Indeed, homeowners often benefit when the value of their land increases (though their real estate taxes are also likely to increase).

---

- **Transit corridors.** Transit (subway and bus) corridors are upzoned. This is known as "Transit-Oriented Development" (TOD), through which the planners promote higher density development at or near mass transit stops. This is presumed to encourage more people to use mass transit and reduce auto use and commuting times, especially in places where mass transit has excess capacity. Since newer buildings tend to be more energy efficient than older buildings, stimulating new construction presumably favors energy savings. TOD is thus considered to be beneficial to the environment and public health if and when it reduces auto use, a major source of air pollution, injuries, and fatalities. Where the existing built environment is low density—single-family homes, low- to mid-rise apartment buildings, and one-story commercial uses—and when transit use is not at full capacity, as measured by numbers of passengers on trains and in stations, the area is considered to be a prime candidate for rezoning. This is one argument behind the rezonings currently proposed in East New York and the South Bronx, among other locations. However, the presumed benefits of TOD in New York City dwindle when we consider that most of the city's population is already living within walking distance of mass transit, most of the city's subways are operating at or close to capacity, the bus system is not expanding, and there are serious deficits in the maintenance and repair of mass transit that result in the longest average commute times of any city in the United States. Zoning in many of these new TODs also permits significant on-site resident parking, contradicting the claims made by planners while satisfying the interests of developers who market their properties to high-income car owners.[7]

An issue that has not been discussed by the city's planners is the potential impact of TOD on communities of color. While the principle of TOD may be valid, its application in New York City has to be evaluated in light of the severe deficits in mass transit. It appears to have been used opportunistically to justify proposed rezonings in communities of color.[8] This pattern has been strongly criticized in other parts of the nation (Fujioka 2011).

---

# ZONING TO SOLVE THE HOUSING PROBLEM? OR AN AFFORDABLE HOUSING SCAM?

One of the great myths circulating around public discussions of zoning is that zoning changes are essential for solving the housing problem. The city's planners sell their zoning schemes by claiming they are necessary to expand the housing stock to meet the needs of a growing population. This echoes the constant criticism heard by the real estate industry that zoning regulations inhibit housing development by limiting the amount of buildable space and increasing costs. The assumption behind this is that the strict market principle of the law of supply and demand is the driving force behind housing development, including affordable housing. This fails to take into account the role of housing subsidies, tax policy and, most importantly, the land market.

For example, Vicki Been, Commissioner of the city's Department of Housing Preservation and Development, testified that the proposed rezoning of East New York to promote new development would actually help solve the crisis of affordable housing in the neighborhood: "The zoning proposal before you today is not the trigger for displacement; instead, it is a preventative measure."[9] She argued that some people were falsely claiming that the rezoning would displace 50,000 people; she clarified that the Draft Environmental Impact Statement submitted with the rezoning proposal stated that 50,000 people were already at risk of displacement. She argued that the new affordable housing was therefore in great need. However, she did not address the fact that the real estate speculation that had placed many people at risk was stimulated by DCP's talk of a rezoning that began some two years prior to the actual proposal. She also made a facile assumption that any new affordable housing would be affordable to those who were displaced, and available in a timely manner.

The myth that growth will solve housing problems was boldly asserted in PlaNYC2030, the pro-growth "sustainability plan" issued in 2007, which claimed that housing had to be built for a projected one million new residents. This dubious premise, based on questionable projections, was the underpinning for the growth plan, which overshadowed every other priority in the plan (Angotti 2008a, 2008b).

It is telling that the first chapter in this "sustainability plan" is "Housing." The bold proposals for growth overwhelm the other sections that call for such embellishments as planting one million new trees, completing the old (1997) bicycle master plan, and creating small public plazas.

Increasingly, the claim about solving the housing problem is folded into the claim that rezoning is needed to provide "affordable housing." As we argue later on, even if the new zoning mandates that a portion of new housing units be "affordable" to people with limited incomes, this number is commonly dwarfed by the number of affordable housing units lost and the new unaffordable units built after an upzoning. Furthermore, some or all of the new affordable units may be built outside the rezoned neighborhoods and reinforce existing patterns of segregation by income and race. Finally, since new affordable housing is available to people in higher income brackets, very few low-income households qualify for these units. Thus, the problem is that the bulk of new housing built after upzonings is for the luxury market,

## SOME NYC PLANNING CHIEFS

**Carl Weisbrod** was named Chair of the City Planning Commission by Mayor Bill de Blasio. He started his career working for the city's Department of Relocation, which was responsible for removing residents and businesses from urban renewal areas. He led the efforts to redevelop Times Square and Lower Manhattan after 9/11. He most recently was a partner in HR&A Advisors, consultant to major development firms.

**Amanda Burden** was Chair of the City Planning Commission during Michael Bloomberg's 12 years as Mayor. Now a Principal at Bloomberg Associates, she is noted for her attention to details of design and public space and promotion of development on the waterfront and in downtown areas. Her father was an heir to the Standard Oil fortune and her stepfather founded CBS.

Other planning commissioners with strong ties to prominent New York City developers include **Joseph Rose** and **John Zuccotti**.

is off-limits to most people living in the neighborhood, and drives up rents and housing costs instead of lowering them. And the few "affordable" housing units made available are not affordable to most existing residents.

# The bulk of new housing built after upzonings is for the luxury market, is off-limits to most people living in the neighborhood, and drives up rents and housing costs instead of lowering them. And the few "affordable" housing units made available are not affordable to most existing residents.

We will return to the larger question of housing affordability later, but our point here is to demonstrate how much the city's land use policies are based on the false premise that zoning can resolve the city's housing problems, particularly housing for the people who need it the most.

# The land market and not the housing market drives housing policy in New York City.

## IT'S THE LAND MARKET, STUPID!

The argument that zoning policy is needed to stimulate the housing market is grounded in a simplistic version of neoclassical economic theory. It presumes that the lack of housing is simply a matter of supply and demand. If there is not enough housing, then government needs to remove any barriers—zoning is presumably one of them—so the market can produce more housing. After all, in many parts of the country with liberal zoning policies, particularly the Southwest, new housing construction boomed while New York City lagged.

This argument obscures the most important factor in New York City's housing market, which is the same factor that governs zoning policy: the land market. Unlike the suburbs of Las Vegas, land in New York City is very expensive and much of it is already developed. Where land is cheap it's quite easy for developers to build (perhaps too easy, since after the housing bust of 2007-2008 many homes in Las Vegas were foreclosed and abandoned). This is why it is the land market and not the housing market that drives land use policy in New York City. Upzoning increases the future value of land, and land value increases are what drives new development.

In New York City, land values change progressively, often in tandem with the different phases of the rezoning process:[10]

- **Phase 1: Land speculation.** When investors find "underutilized" parcels of land, they move in and buy them up or secure options to buy. They may be able to assemble adjacent parcels on one block or on many blocks. They often register the deeds under different Limited Liability Corporations (LLCs), making it difficult to understand the emerging patterns of ownership. During this phase the land value remains low but once it becomes clear that land is being assembled for possible future development the value may increase as investors engage in a buying frenzy. Landowners may also terminate leases to remove existing residents and businesses and issue short-term leases to new businesses with higher rents. These interim uses, such as storage and parking facilities, are essentially placeholders for new development that will occur after a rezoning.

---

• *Phase 2: Department of City Planning study.* Property owners and others may bring the situation of de facto underutilized land to the attention of DCP. DCP may already be aware of the situation. Indeed, DCP's institutional brain is wired to think like a land developer and be alert for opportunities for new growth. DCP then undertakes a land use study. They usually do not do a study unless they are reasonably certain they will be proposing a rezoning. This in itself is quite revealing: the agency uses studies not to determine what a community needs, but to shape the particular contours of an expected rezoning. These are not planning studies that look at the community in all its complexity; they are not really land use studies that look at land as a complex set of relationships in urban space. They are narrowly focused on zoning. DCP zoning studies calculate the square feet of existing land and building space and then determine whether a zoning change is needed to develop the underutilized parcels. Typically DCP will consult with the local community board before, during, and after it does the study; however, community boards are usually reminded that this consultation is merely a courtesy since community board votes are "advisory." DCP studies lead inexorably from a finding of significant underutilization to a conclusion that a rezoning is needed. While the DCP study is underway, land values are likely to increase in anticipation of a rezoning; in other words, DCP's actions play a role in creating the circumstances that justify rezoning. When developers get wind that DCP might be studying a neighborhood for rezoning, they start to move in. Crain's reported that in East New York (Brooklyn), since the city administration started pushing for a rezoning in early 2015 "prices and sales volume have begun to rise." The median sales price for a home in the main zip code rose from $25,500 to $275,000—a tenfold increase (Acitelli, 2016)!

- **Phase 3: Rezoning Proposal.** DCP has monopoly control over the zoning process and the substance of zoning changes. The CPC must certify that all zoning proposals are complete, and they do this at the recommendation of the DCP staff. All rezoning proposals must be accompanied by an environmental review that meets the approval of DCP staff. In practice, rezonings are initiated either by DCP or by private developers or landowners. Because of the time and resources required, community groups and individual residents rarely initiate a rezoning. Even when a community board requests a rezoning, DCP does the study and shapes the proposal. Reluctant community boards may again be reminded that their vote is only advisory.

---

- **Phase 4. The ULURP process.** The Uniform Land Use Review Procedure (ULURP) is about seven months long and involves public hearings and votes by the local community board, borough president, CPC, and city council, and on occasion the mayor.[11] While community boards are the closest of these bodies to the neighborhood being rezoned, they have the least power. A unanimous vote by a community board in opposition to a rezoning is not enough to kill it. Community boards do not have professional planners on their staff to advise them, analyze environmental studies, or prepare their own zoning proposals. Boards with access to more resources often find that their recommendations are also ignored.[12] Promises the city may make to community boards during the process—to provide community benefits such as affordable housing, or new public facilities and services, even when they are drafted as a "side agreement"—are of dubious legal value and unenforceable (see Chapter Three). Given the limitations of the ULURP process, once a rezoning proposal supported by DCP starts ULURP, it is virtually a "done deal" unless the city council, borough president,and community board all vote against it. This often leads community boards to vote "yes" or "no" with conditions in the hopes that their conditions will be met in the final negotiations leading up to the virtually inevitable city council approval. It is significant that every one of Mayor Bloomberg's rezoning proposals (described below) were approved.

# THE BLOOMBERG ZONING BLITZ

Under the administration of Mayor Michael Bloomberg (2002–2014), the city undertook a major rezoning campaign. Some 37 percent of the land in the city was rezoned, the largest set of rezonings ever, through almost 140 separate zoning actions.[13] As shown in Figure 1.B, many of these rezonings were instituted during the real estate boom preceding the 2007-2008 bust. This rash of rezonings was consistent with the mayor's pro-growth agenda and long-term sustainability plan, which called for the development of new housing for a population expected to grow by one million people before the year 2030 (City of New York 2007). The analysis by Leo Goldberg divides the rezoning actions into *upzonings*, which are aimed at increasing development capacity, *downzonings* that preserve existing development, and *hybrid* rezonings that combine both actions.

The vast majority of the rezonings protected areas throughout the five boroughs. The Bloomberg administration chose to undertake this substantial rezoning campaign instead of a comprehensive revision of the Zoning Resolution—perhaps a worthy endeavor to consider since over a half-century had passed since the last one. It is even more remarkable that the city chose to propose many localized, smaller zoning changes instead of engaging communities in a process of comprehensive long-term planning. All of this suggests that the allegiance to zoning over planning is deeply imbedded in the political culture of New York City.

# ZONING AND RACE

The 15 rezoning plans currently advanced by Mayor de Blasio include large areas in East New York, the South Bronx, Flushing, and East Harlem, all communities of color. They squarely raise the question of the impact of the rezonings on racial minorities, not always evident during the Bloomberg years because of the large number of rezonings, the variety of neighborhoods affected, and the wide variation in types and scale of rezonings. While some of Mayor Bloomberg's rezonings faced intense neighborhood opposition and charges of racial bias, such as the rezoning of 125th Street in Harlem, many of the Bloomberg-era rezonings had the effect of preserving existing communities, or mixing preservation with limited upzoning, they generally faced limited, though often vocal, opposition. Every one of them was approved. Race was not a major item for discussion—especially when it came to the rezonings in middle- and upper-income neighborhoods which are disproportionately white.

Up until now, we have barely mentioned race when discussing zoning. This is, in effect, the way many city planners are taught to understand land use and zoning, as "race-neutral." The DCP has never seriously broached the question or produced a study of the racial implications of zoning laws or the agency's own practices. It appears that zoning, like many other areas of public policy, is dealt with as "color blind" and part of the mythical "post-racial society."[14]

# Many city planners are taught to understand land use and zoning as 'race neutral.'

However, in a study of 76 rezonings between 2003 and 2007, the NYU Furman Center found that "upzoned lots tended to be located in census tracts with a higher proportion of non-white residents than the median tract in the city." More particularly, these areas had higher concentrations of African American and Hispanic residents than the city median (Furman Center 2010).

Looking at income, the Furman Center study found that upzoned lots were in areas with "significantly lower income" and "much lower home-ownership rates" than the city median. Downzoned lots tended to be in areas that had income levels and home ownership rates below the city median but above those in upzoned areas. In contrast, contextual zoning occurred in areas where income and homeownership levels were much higher than the city median (Furman Center 2010). Recent research covering most of the Bloomberg-era rezonings, which occurred between 2003 and 2013, suggests that the Furman Center's findings were broadly valid, although the collapse of the land market in 2007–2008 makes it difficult to draw definitive conclusions. Many upzonings and hybrid rezonings did not have a measurable immediate impact due to the decline in the real estate market (Goldberg 2015).

Rezonings in strategic areas in and near the highest value real estate in the city, however, have had clear, significant impacts on communities of color. Chapters three through five present three very dramatic case studies of neighborhoods that have seen swift change and racially disparate displacement—Williamsburg (Brooklyn), and Harlem and Chinatown in

## 01.B Department of City Planning-Rezonings by Year, 2003–2013

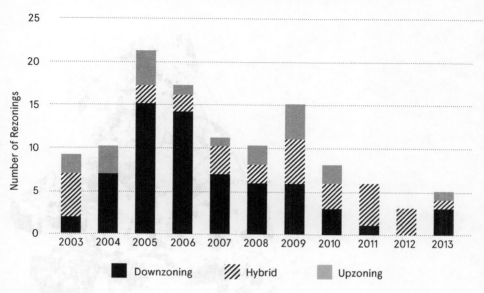

Leo Goldberg (2015).

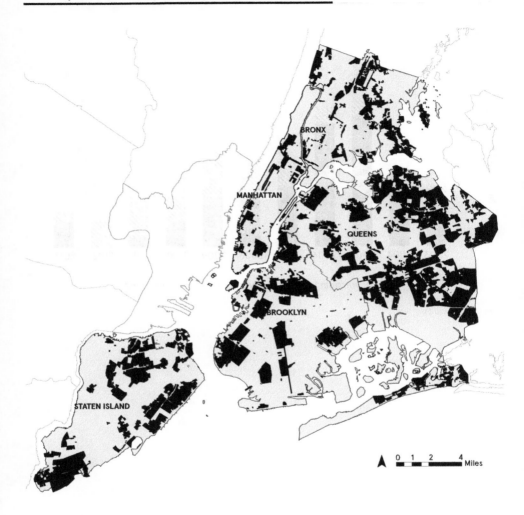

0 1 2 4 Miles

■ Zoning Amendments

New York City Department of City Planning, NYC GIS Zoning Features December 2015.

Manhattan. These cases show how rezonings have resulted in the displacement of minorities by stimulating new development that prices them out or by failing to provide zoning protections when they are most needed. In each case, the city failed to consider the likelihood of displacement and the ways it might affect minority populations.

# DISPLACEMENT

From the perspective of the city's pro-growth strategists, displacement is not a major problem. For residents, community-based organizations, and small businesses, it is a critical problem. While public officials may acknowledge neighborhood concerns, there has been no serious action dealing with displacement. If it were seen as a problem, it would be a widely reported subject of debate in government circles and the press. There would be studies that sought to understand whether displacement occurred after a rezoning, who was displaced, and where they went. There would be well-funded committees and task forces with enforcement powers. None of this exists.[15]

It would appear that displacement is understood as one of those unavoidable consequences of development—in much the same way that Robert Moses declared, in defense of his projects that displaced people, "you can't make an omelette without breaking eggs" (Caro 1975). A common argument in defense of gentrification and displacement is that change is a constant and those raising questions about it are part of a chronic knee-jerk reaction against any change. Or, just expressions of nostalgia for what exists (Lees, Slater and Wyly 2008; Smith and Williams 1986).

From the perspective of "trickle-down" housing economics, there really is no downside to new development and anyone raising questions is merely interfering with the free market, which, we are told, will work its miracles if left alone. Ultimately, say the free-marketeers, new development benefits low-income and minority communities because the increased supply of luxury, market-rate housing units will free up existing units for people with lower incomes as everyone moves up along the chain connecting all income brackets. In a perverse twist, they argue that the people raising the issue of displacement are actually undermining the creation of housing for low-income minorities.

This is a fantastical story. It is the fable that underlies the city's land use and zoning policies. This is how it really works: new market-rate housing units principally serve the luxury market and the existing housing units don't trickle down. The relatively high rate of vacancies in luxury buildings

# WHAT IS DISPLACEMENT?
# HOW DOES IT HAPPEN IN NEW YORK CITY?

People all over the city are talking about displacement, in
private conversations and public hearings. Displacement is not
only about people moving from one place to another, but also large
numbers of people having to move and having little choice in the
matter. It is about people being forced out by rising land prices
and rents, which is happening all over the city to a greater or
lesser degree. It can happen as part of a gradual gentrification
process, or it can be connected to rapid changes sparked by large-
scale development and rezoning. Residents, housing activists,
and legal advocates in the city tell stories of long-time tenants
forced to move due to rising rents and landlord harassment.

Displacement affects many white neighborhoods as well as
communities of color. However, whites typically are much more
mobile and can take advantage of many affordable alternative
housing opportunities. For low-income communities and communities
of color, the alternatives are much more limited due to widespread
discrimination in the housing and real estate markets. In the
neighborhoods they are forced to leave, the new residents and
businesses tend to be wealthier and whiter.

While New Yorkers may intuitively know or directly experience
displacement, the city has done little to measure or prevent it.
No city, state, or federal agency documents residential turnover
and the extent to which it may disproportionately affect people
by income and race. City agencies responsible for land use and
housing policy do not collect information about the effect of
their policies and programs on residential stability, never asking
who might be displaced, where they might go, and whether they face
better or worse living conditions. Without this data, community-
based organizations concerned about displacement have limited
information with which to combat it, and city government lacks the
basic facts needed to either counter or mitigate displacement.

For a start, these are five major kinds of displacement that need
to be addressed:

**1. Rent-stabilized tenants.** Rent regulation limits rent
increases and guarantees the right to lease renewal. In the
last decade, more than 50,000 rent-stabilized housing units
were lost because landlords illegally forced tenants out,
or paid them to leave so they could rent to people with much
higher incomes, or the units were no longer stabilized because
rents skyrocketed above the maximum that warrants protection.

**2. Market-rate tenants.** Tenants in buildings with five units
or less, and most large buildings built after 1974, do not have
the protections of rent-stabilized tenants. When owners sell
to investors or flippers, tenants are often evicted or handed
substantial rent increases.

**3. Homeowner displacement.** Homeowners in and around rezoning
areas face intense pressure to sell their properties.
Fraudulent foreclosure relief companies target many elderly
and financially struggling owners while others are victimized
by deed theft. Companies looking to flip these properties
often convince homeowners to sell far below the real value
of their homes and then turn around and sell at much higher
prices. Predatory lending practices, concentrated in
communities of color, result in displacement and free up
property for speculative redevelopment.

**4. Small business displacement.** Small businesses have no rent
protections and are vulnerable to steep rent increases when a
landlord chooses to capitalize on the influx of new residents
with higher buying power in a neighborhood. Often, corporate-
owned businesses replace locally owned businesses, further
homogenizing life in the city's neighborhoods.

**5. Industrial displacement.** Much of the city's industrial
zoning leaves manufacturing and industrial uses open to
competition from hotel, office and commercial uses that
command higher rents. Speculators often move in before a
neighborhood changes and wait for land values to skyrocket and
then lobby for a zoning change.

belies the notion that the surplus will trickle down to poor people; it simply remains at the top as landowners hold out for higher prices and rents. At the same time, the lack of affordable housing for low- and moderate-income households remains constant because "the market" does not build for them, and government subsidies are simply not sufficient to fill the gap. This has been further complicated by the withdrawal of direct public subsidies from low-income housing starting in the 1980s as part of the neoliberal turn in public policy aimed at unleashing the full power of the "free market." In the end, the new luxury housing produced by the market forces more people into the existing housing stock, which, if you follow the theory of supply and demand, means that the rents there will actually go up and not down!

A few examples from the city's history are useful counters to the free market narrative, as they reflect major long-term trends. In 19th-century Manhattan, the expansion of uptown housing for the gentry coincided with a severe housing shortage and overcrowded tenements. The building boom of the 1950s and 1960s was followed by massive housing abandonment in the 1970s. Throughout the city's history, homelessness and overcrowding have been a constant and have grown during building booms. We can see this happening at the neighborhood level when new development drives up land values and rents in surrounding blocks and tenants in the buildings on these blocks can't afford to pay higher rents and are forced out. They end up in the limited stock of increasingly overcrowded affordable housing or, perhaps, in homeless shelters or on the streets.

The long-term trends are repeated in short-term changes tied to rezonings. According to research by Leo Goldberg, between 2002 and 2013, the city's rezoning program produced immense value for landowners. Property values in upzoned areas rapidly increased in comparison to other parts of the city. Lots with dense building types appreciated particularly fast: the assessed value of multi-family buildings in upzoned areas increased by 120 percent while mixed-use buildings increased by 100 percent. Neighborhoods subject to hybrid rezonings produced value increases that were nearly as large. The increased valuations of multi-family buildings result in higher property taxes; in rental buildings, these are passed on to tenants in the form of higher rents (Goldberg 2015).

These results are consistent with the findings of an NYU Furman Center study that found that "just 26 percent of units constructed since 2000 rented for $1,005 or less in 2012, a level affordable to the median renter household" (Furman Center 2013, 34). However, even at this rent level, such housing is not affordable to the majority of people living in the neighborhoods that were rezoned for new development.

Upzoned areas, where new high-end housing units were built, predictably increased the rent burden on households in these areas, as stated in a report by the NYC Comptroller:

> It is reasonable to expect that if the number of middle- or high-income households in a neighborhood increases, so will average rents and home prices. New housing development, typically of a higher cost than the existing housing stock, will usually become more viable and common. There will be more competition for existing housing units and more income available to monetize that competition (Stringer2014, 16).

At the end of the day, increases in "affordable housing" lag far behind the increases in market-rate housing. From 2002 to 2012, "while income-restricted subsidized stock grew by about 12 percent, the market-rate stock grew by much more, increasing by 28 percent" (Furman Center 2013, 36). Further, new rent-stabilized units built in exchange for property tax benefits may (and often do) rent at levels that increase to above the "deregulation threshold, currently $2,700 per month, after which rents are no longer regulated" (Furman Center 2013, 34).

# RACE AND THE MARKET, ZONING AND FAIR HOUSING

Beyond the myths of market magic there resides the myth of race neutrality—the notion that the land market, housing market, and the zoning that regulates them have nothing to do with racial discrimination or segregation.

DCP's reliance on zoning as the main instrument of land use policy makes it difficult to challenge the myth. The city's multi-volume Zoning Resolution is complex and constantly changing, and most New Yorkers have to rely on technical experts to interpret it for them. There is nothing in the Zoning Resolution about race. There is not a hint that this is a city of segregated neighborhoods and schools, or that race might figure in the formulation of land use and zoning policy. There is not even a serious public dialogue about what race might have to do with the way the city uses its zoning powers.

The 1968 Fair Housing Act prohibits discrimination in housing. It bans local government policies that have a discriminatory effect as well as intentional acts of racial bias. In New York City it would be hard to find examples of blatant acts of intentional racial bias in zoning and planning, simply because race is not usually mentioned.

If it is not talked about then it is difficult to ferret out any discriminatory intent. However, it is certainly possible to assess whether zoning actions have a discriminatory effect.

The city has never seriously looked at the potential discriminatory impact of its rezonings. Since it does not recognize displacement as a major contributor to segregation and racial disparities, it does not track and measure displacement resulting from its own actions. It is worth repeating: there has never been a study of how many people were displaced by rezonings, where they went, whether they are better off or not, and whether their new living conditions are better or worse. Unless we know what happens when people are displaced, how can the city's planners make informed decisions? How can they know whether a rezoning has a disparate impact on people of different races, ethnicities and incomes, as many residents suspect? How can residents make informed decisions about whether to support or reject rezonings?

# The city has never seriously looked at the potential discriminatory impact of its rezonings.

At times, city officials point to the environmental impact analyses that accompany zoning proposals. These include a section on social and economic impacts, which may involve an analysis of existing income and racial groups, and estimate the number of people who will be directly and indirectly displaced by a rezoning. The analysis tends to be buried in large and unwieldy documents that are filed with the zoning applications but rarely get in-depth scrutiny. Community boards do not have the time or professional assistance needed to plow through and challenge them. Few elected officials give them a critical review.

However, even those who care to read and challenge the environmental review cannot reject it because the environmental review is mainly intended to disclose potential negative impacts, and there is no requirement that the applicant revise or withdraw their application. Mitigations may be promised in the environmental reviews but there is rarely sufficient enforcement to insure that they are implemented. In sum, environmental review is a weak, underutilized tool for understanding the disparate impact of displacement resulting from zoning.

The better alternative would be a thorough, in-depth analysis of different kinds of zoning actions over time, in different neighborhoods throughout the city. For this analysis the city will need to consistently monitor and measure displacement by race and ethnicity throughout the city.

The city's "color blindness" is not simply a transitory disease. It is a chronic element resulting from many decades of discrimination going back to the very founding of the city and the nation. New York City does not stand alone in this. In some ways it has been exemplary in providing housing for low-income and minority people and rejecting the exclusionary zoning and land use practices of the suburbs in the New York metropolitan region. However, in the following chapters we will show that the city, driven by its dynamic real estate market, has evolved unique forms of racial exclusion and discrimination, abetted by zoning and housing policies.

**Endnotes**

1. Under the Lindsay administration, city planners produced a "master plan," which underwent contentious public hearings, faced intense criticism by civic and planning groups, and faced lawsuits between 1969 and 1972. It was never voted on or approved, but was "put aside," according to city planning officials.

   Paul Goldberger, "Why City Is Switching From Master Plan to 'Miniplan,'" *The New York Times*, June 27, 1974.

2. Parks are outlined on zoning maps but not subject to zoning.

3. The Zoning Resolution is at http://www.nyc.gov/html/dcp/html/subcats/zoning.shtml; for a comprehensive history and discussion see Bressi 1993.

4. See http://www.nyc.gov/html/dcp/home.html.

   City agencies and independent groups have developed a number of educational resources to help the public and independent professionals understand zoning tools and existing city zoning rules. New York City Department of City Planning, *New York City Zoning Handbook*, 2011 Edition (City of New York, 2011); Christine Gaspar, Mark Torrey, and John Mangin, "What is Zoning?" Center for Urban Pedagogy, 2013, Accessed January 23, 2016, http://welcometocup.org/file_columns/0000/0530/cup-whatiszoning-guidebook.pdf.

5. As elsewhere, this section relies on the author's decades of experience with land use, zoning, and housing in New York City and eight years as a senior planner with the City of New York. The types of zoning are general and the result of an interpretation that attempts to extract the main trends. They are grounded in the detailed research of Goldberg 2015. DCP does not formally categorize its rezonings in this way.

6. Often DCP finds that there are also "overbuilt" lots that exceed the floor area allowed under the existing zoning, perhaps because they were built before the city's zoning rules were first instituted in 1916, or before they were substantially revised in 1961. These are considered "non-complying" lots. Wherever possible the DCP will upzone these lots so that the buildings comply with the zoning, or include them in a wider upzoning. This type of upzoning to increase compliance does not always spark redevelopment, especially if it occurs on a small scale and is not part of a much wider rezoning.

7. The Atlantic Yards development in Brooklyn, located at the third largest transit hub in the city, is a prime example.

8. At the time of this writing, the Department of City Planning is currently engaging in a number of neighborhood studies and rezonings, including the East New York rezoning and Jerome Avenue neighborhood study.

   "East New York Community Planning," the Department of City Planning, accessed January 23, 2016, http://www.nyc.gov/html/dcp/html/east_new_york/index.shtml.

   "Jerome Avenue Study," the Department of City Planning, accessed January 23, 2016, http://www.nyc.gov/html/dcp/html/jerome_ave/index.shtml.

9. Jarrett Murphy, "De Blasio Housing Chief Rebuts Critics of East N.Y. Plan," *City Limits*, January 7, 2016, http://citylimits.org/2016/01/07/de-blasio-housing-chief-rebuts-critics-of-east-n-y-plan.

   These phases are not always neatly separated, and land values may increase at vastly different rates, depending on the circumstances of time and place. The phases are an interpretation that we hope will help outsiders understand how zoning and development really work in the real world. See also endnote 3.

11. See "Applicant Portal: UNIFORM LAND USE REVIEW PROCEDURE (ULURP)," Department of City Planning, accessed January 23, 2016, http://www.nyc.gov/html/dcp/html/ap/step5_ulurp.shtml.

12. Manhattan Community Board 2, for instance, unanimously vetoed a New York University rezoning and development plan in 2012, and included detailed analysis and recommendations, which were largely unaddressed in subsequent ULURP review and the final approval by CPC and the City Council.

    Community Board No. 2, Manhattan, "Re: NYU Core Project; ULURP Applications Nos.: 120122 ZMM, N 120123 ZRM, N 120124 ZSM, 120077 MMM," March 11, 2012, accessed January 23, 2016, http://www.nyc.gov/html/mancb2/downloads/pdf/nyu_ulurp_response_approved%20 2_23_2012.pdf

13. A group calling itself "Appreciative New Yorkers" took out a full-page ad in *The New York Times* on December 28, 2013, praising Bloomberg for, among many other things, rezoning 37 percent of the city.

14. During my years working as a senior planner with DCP I heard top managers claim that zoning is "race neutral," in response to questions raised about the impacts of zoning on minority communities. Listening today to the stories of the state officials who failed to acknowledge the extreme contamination of the Flint, Michigan, water supply for a year and a half, it seems obvious that there is serious case of color-blindness at work with consequences that have proved to be devastating and even fatal for many residents of the mostly black city of Flint.

15. The New York State Tenant Protection Unit, introduced in 2011, and Tenant Harassment Prevention Task Force, launched in 2015, are aimed at cracking down on landlords who violate the rent regulations, including illegal rent increases and tenant harassment. These efforts may best be described as too little and too late. In places like East New York, currently proposed for upzoning, many tenants live in housing units not covered by the rent regulations and many have already been displaced in the speculative fever leading up to the public release of the rezoning proposal.

# CHAPTER TWO

# RACIALIZED LAND USE AND HOUSING POLICIES

## TOM ANGOTTI AND SYLVIA MORSE[1]

Over the last century, through its land use, zoning, and housing policies New York City followed and reinforced national policies and local market trends that have contributed to racial inequality and segregation. In this chapter we will briefly outline this history. While certainly not exhaustive, the purpose of this review is to demonstrate that local policies have for a long time contributed to racial discrimination and displacement because the city has failed to use its powers to confront market forces and federal policies that reinforce economic and racial inequalities, and in many cases has collaborated with them. The evidence adds up to proof that gentrification and displacement are not natural, independent and benevolent phenomena. The case studies in chapters three through five demonstrate how the city's current policies fail to break with the long history, and the final chapter outlines suggestions for doing so.

## ZONING INSTEAD OF PLANNING

New York City's 1811 grid plan was the first major effort to rationalize land development and created Manhattan's well-know pattern of development along avenues running north and south, and streets running east and west. This was quite useful for large landowners who subdivided their land to sell off house lots, most of which went to white buyers. The next great exercise in planning was the creation of Central Park, which resulted in the displacement of poor whites and blacks (Rosenzweig and Blackmar 1997). But, as the city's population exploded in the early 20th century, concern arose among downtown property owners that the value of their commercial property and housing would be dragged down by the growth of industry and the tenements that housed their workers. This led to the establishment of zoning regulations in 1916. Like the 1811 grid plan, zoning was supported by large property owners and the budding real estate industry.

Significantly, New York City preferred zoning over comprehensive planning—a critical choice whose importance would become more apparent many decades later when neighborhoods began to call for community planning. Comprehensive planning takes a look at prospects for the long-term future of the city and sets out policies to help shape that future, integrating all aspects of the city's physical, economic, and social development and preservation. Zoning was used in a way that downplayed long-term planning and emphasized physical development over questions of economic and social well-being. From the start, it was not race or class neutral, as we show in this chapter.

**36**

New York City is the only major city in the United States that has never approved a comprehensive (master) plan. This is not an incidental oversight; it is a direct reflection of the power of the real estate industry, which prefers to rely on individual, localized deals that can be synchronized with zoning changes without having to justify its relationship to any broad city-wide strategy that may be subject to more extensive political debate.

### RACIAL ZONING

A major rationale for zoning was that it would help improve living conditions. In the late 19th century, an active civic reform movement pressed for regulations to improve housing and sanitary conditions that contributed to serious epidemics that especially affected working-class neighborhoods. The 1916 zoning ordinance regulated building height and density to allow for more light and air, which were lacking in many older tenement houses that were breeding deadly epidemics. However, by the time zoning was introduced, a series of tenement laws had already outlawed the construction of housing with unsafe and unsanitary conditions. The emphasis on light and air promoted the notion that taller buildings resulting in higher densities were in the public interest and the answer to gritty industries and working class housing. The new development spurred by zoning also created profitable opportunities for landowners. Zoning, like the 1811 grid plan, was mainly presented as a mechanism to create orderly growth, but with regulations that went beyond minimal controls over the subdivision of land into blocks and lots.

A fundamental principle of the new zoning was the segregation of uses—industrial, commercial and residential. Much of the city beyond lower Manhattan allowed for a mixture of uses, giving flexibility to developers who subdivided land around the city's new subway lines. However, in the developed core, the precedent was set for segregating land uses as a means of promoting social and racial exclusion.

# ZONING, SEGREGATION, AND DISPLACEMENT

After Reconstruction in 1877, cities around the country began experimenting first with racial ordinances and then the emerging practice of zoning to limit the expansion of black people in white residential areas (Brooks and Rose, 24). Baltimore was the first to create a comprehensive zoning ordinance that made it illegal for black people to move to a block where more than half the residents were white, and vice versa. Fourteen other cities

# SLAVERY AND THE UNDERGROUND RAILROAD IN NEW YORK CITY

A superficial reading of history portrays New York City as a strong liberal bastion of opposition to slavery and racism. However, slavery was legal in New York State until 1827 and, according to historian Eric Foner, "New York had close economic ties to the slave South and a pro-southern municipal government [...] Even after slavery ended in New York, the South's peculiar institution remained central to the city's economic prosperity" (Foner 2015). Nevertheless, New York City became a major destination for free black people. Those who ended up living in the city could initially find housing in and near white working-class neighborhoods. However, violent racial attacks, such as the infamous Draft Riots of 1863, and a dramatic increase in migration from Europe, led to the eventual formation of segregated black neighborhoods by the early 20th century.

After the Civil War and the abolition of slavery, black people in the rural south toiled under a system of sharecropping and were terrorized by physical violence. Reconstruction was ended after barely a decade, and the Great Migration to cities began, first within the south, and then to the north. Although there were racial and ethnic clusters in northern cities, black residents rarely comprised more than 30 percent of any one area, and these were distributed throughout cities, a pattern shared by European immigrants. A typical black resident of a 19th-century northern city lived in a neighborhood that was roughly 90 percent white. This was not a sign of racial integration, but of the preponderance of whites in a relatively small city where blacks were nonetheless second-class citizens because of their economic status and exposure to violence (Massey and Denton 1993, 17-24).

This changed dramatically in the 20th century. In the 1910s, 525,000 black people migrated north; in the 1920s the number was 877,000 (Massey and Denton 1993, 27-29). In New York City, black neighborhoods in Midtown became overcrowded as land values and rents there exploded. Black people were displaced by the forces of real estate speculation to then-predominantly white Harlem (Brooks and Rose 2014, 24). In 1910, the entire black population of the city was 60,534, and by 1914 approximately 50,000 black people were living in Harlem.

followed suit—mostly but not entirely southern cities—by hiring urban planners to design policies designating separate areas where blacks and whites could live, by withholding building permits, and establishing commercial or industrial buffers to separate residential areas between the races. In 1917, one year after New York City's zoning ordinance took effect, the Supreme Court in *Buchanan v. Warley* declared racial zoning unconstitutional, ruling against a white property owner in Louisville who argued the ordinance violated his right to sell to a buyer of his choice under the Fourteenth Amendment (Pietila 2010, 23; Rabin 1989, 106; Taylor 2014, 151, 157).

Unlike many southern and suburban municipalities, New York City never incorporated explicit racial exclusions in its zoning regulations. This does not mean, however, that zoning has not been used to reinforce racial segregation that resulted from discrimination in the housing and real estate sectors.

## RACIAL COVENANTS

In many places, covenants written into deeds prevented owners and their heirs from selling or renting to a black person for generations. These restrictive covenants explicitly excluded black people until a landmark Supreme Court ruling in 1948 ruled against the practice.

Racial and other restrictive covenants were used in parts of New York City and the suburbs to keep middle-class black families from moving into white areas. A 1947 study examining 300 suburban-style developments in Queens, Nassau, and southern Westchester County found covenants included in 48 percent of subdivisions with 20 homes or more, and in 80 percent of subdivisions with 75 homes or more. After 1938, when the Federal Housing Administration (FHA) began recommending 25 to 30-year racial covenants as a condition of funding in its Underwriting Manual, all subdivisions in the study contained them (Dean 1947). The Supreme Court ruled in the 1948 case, *Shelley v. Kramer*, that racial covenants were illegal and the FHA later stopped insuring mortgages subject to racial covenants (Jackson 2008, 208). However, many of these covenants remained in place decades after the Supreme Court ruling, some even into the 21st century (Brooks and Rose 2013, 229).

## EXCLUSIONARY ZONING

As racial zoning and restrictive covenants were gradually invalidated by courts, subtler forms of exclusion emerged. Zoning became the main legally defensible means for communities to segregate under the guise of a public interest in protecting the health, safety, and welfare of people, though this was often framed as protecting property values or "neighborhood character." Suburban communities have used exclusionary zoning—and continue to this day—to restrict the building of housing that is affordable and amenable to the needs of racial minorities. Exclusionary zoning ordinances typically establish a minimum lot size or maximum density, require large setbacks and yards, limit or prevent multi-family housing, and ban mobile or prefabricated homes (Taylor 2014, 184–185). Zoning can be used along with excessive taxes and fees, extensive design reviews, and infrastructure requirements to make it impossible to build housing affordable to low-income people; given the racial disparities in incomes between blacks and whites, exclusionary zoning effectively discriminates against people of color. Exclusionary zoning in suburbs has also kept out certain kinds of industrial and commercial development that would increase the need for low-income workers and the places where they could be housed.

While exclusionary zoning is usually thought of as a strictly suburban phenomenon, elements of New York City's zoning have always been exclusionary. The 1916 zoning resolution mainly regulated land use in the more developed upscale core of Manhattan, where industrial uses and new tenement houses, and the low-income immigrant communities associated with them, were excluded. A laissez-faire approach in the outer boroughs allowed market trends to shape development there, along with the discriminatory sales and rental practices used by some developers and landlords. The 1961 zoning extended the separation of uses in zoning throughout the five boroughs.

While exclusionary zoning is usually thought of as a strictly suburban phenomenon, elements of New York City's zoning have always been exclusionary.

One of the patterns that persisted after the 1961 zoning changes and through the rest of the century was that areas zoned for relatively low densities—New York City's internal "suburbs"—protected the largely

Zoned Out!

white homeowners who lived there. These included large parts of eastern Queens, the North Bronx, southern Brooklyn, and most of Staten Island.

These exclusionary areas have diminished over the years as soaring land values rippled out beyond Manhattan and led to the construction of higher density enclaves in all of the boroughs. However, the pattern remains in place as a number of low-density, predominantly white enclaves continue to be protected by zoning. Over the last two decades, some of these white neighborhoods (for example parts of Flatbush in Brooklyn) gave way to homeowners from non-white immigrant populations, who have for a while benefited from the exclusionary zoning policies they inherited—until intense real estate speculation, in the absence of more protective zoning, began to force them out.

Many white neighborhoods have promoted and defended low-density and contextual zoning. For example, the battles against new apartment development in Forest Hills, Queens, are legendary (Cuomo 1974). While at times racial fears were expressed openly in public meetings, exclusionary sentiments were usually clouded by rhetoric defending the existing low-rise character of neighborhoods. The Department of City Planning (DCP) obliged and reinforced these sentiments with their zoning policies, including the creation of low-density contextual zoning and special preservation districts.

*Special preservation districts* were created to protect areas from development. These include the Special Hillsides Preservation District and Special Natural Area District in Staten Island; the Special City Island District and the Special Natural Area District in north Bronx; and in Queens, the Special Natural Area District in Fort Totten. The Special Forest Hills District was the precedent, created decades ago to protect one of the most distinctive white enclaves of luxury homes in Queens.

*Low-density contextual zoning* (generally in R1–R5 residential zones) has been generously employed throughout the city's "suburban" fringes. In the 1990s, large parts of white Borough Park,[2] in Brooklyn, benefited from a form of contextual zoning that legalized widespread home expansions that had violated zoning and building codes. Instead of contemplating a rezoning that would encourage new higher density residential development—and possible racial change—DCP opted to bend its rules to accommodate this politically powerful white ethnic enclave.

Perhaps one of the most prominent models for contextual zoning was in Brooklyn's Park Slope, where it was used to protect neighborhood scale and character. This low- to mid-rise neighborhood in Brooklyn, next to Prospect Park, prominently features many attractive brownstone blocks. The first of these to be protected were in the relatively affluent white

▲ 0 1 2 4 Miles

Low Density Residential
Zoning Districts (R1–R5)

More than 50% white

U.S. Census Bureau, American Community Survey, 2014 5-year Estimates.
New York City Department of City Planning, NYC Zoning Districts, December 2015.

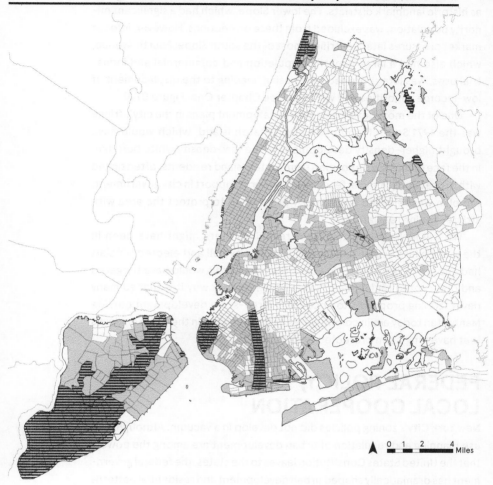

▲ 0 1 2 4 Miles

▨ Special Purpose Districts/
Low Density Preservation

▩ More than 50% white

U.S. Census Bureau, American Community Survey, 2014 5-year Estimates.
New York City Department of City Planning, NYC Zoning Districts, December 2015.

portion of the neighborhood, where many blocks also gained protections as historic landmark districts. The lower Slope, which had a significant minority population, was excluded from these protections. However, intense market pressures later gentrified most of the south Slope. Fourth Avenue, which also had a large minority population and commercial and industrial uses, was later upzoned for housing, leading to the displacement of low-income minorities and workers. (See Chapter One, Figure 01.A)

One of the most hotly contested development plans in the city's fringe was the 1971 South Richmond Plan in Staten Island, which would have brought higher-density development to the low-density white borough. In the face of intense opposition from Staten Island residents, often tinged with expressions of racial fears, and lukewarm support in city government, the plan was rejected and the city proceeded to protect the area with stricter zoning regulations.

We will never know how many rezonings there might have been in the city's white "suburban fringe" if DCP, city hall and elected officials had chosen to ignore the blowback their proposals would have triggered and confronted racial fears. However, we can ask why it is that so many new rezoning proposals to encourage large-scale development outside Manhattan today are in communities of color and not in the white enclaves that have long been protected by zoning.

# FEDERAL POLICY, LOCAL COOPERATION

New York City's zoning policies did not develop in a vacuum. Although land use planning and regulation of urban development are among the powers that the United States Constitution leaves to the states, the federal government has dramatically shaped urban development and residential patterns of US cities. Federal policy, with the city's support, has contributed to racial segregation. Enforcement of fair housing rules has been largely ineffective in countering it in a way that would significantly alter local practices.

After World War II, federal housing and infrastructure programs promoted the dramatic growth of metropolitan areas through the interstate highway program, the largest public works project ever undertaken in the world, and federally guaranteed mortgage financing. This produced the sharp division between central cities, disproportionately black and poor, and suburbs, disproportionately white and middle class, which was famously noted in the 1968 Kerner Commission Report (Report of the National Advisory Commission on Civil Disorders 1968). White suburban

**44**

communities utilized their planning and zoning powers to exclude new development that might provide housing opportunities for low-income people of color. At the same time, central city governments used federal housing and urban renewal programs to limit the opportunities for mobility of poor communities of color. While some state and federal court rulings have placed restrictions on discriminatory zoning and housing policies, the status quo established by federal policy, with the collusion of state and local governments, remains in force. In sum, our racially segregated cities, far from being the result of cultural attitudes or uncontrolled market forces, were largely shaped by federal, state and local policies. According to John Bauman:

> Between 1900 and 1950, the involvement of the federal government in housing significantly increased. At the beginning of the century, housing reformers were divided over the concept of direct federal involvement in the housing market. Two world wars, the Great Depression, and the postwar veterans' housing shortage resulted in a shift of public opinion in favor of federal involvement in housing. By mid-century, there was no longer any question of whether the federal government would intervene in the private housing market—debate focused on which groups of Americans would get housing aid, how much, and in what form (Bauman 2000, xxxv).

During the Great Depression, Congress created a series of New Deal programs to stimulate home building industries, protect families from foreclosure, and address the decline of inner city housing, but in all of these endeavors it managed to work with local governments to disproportionately benefit white homeowners and strengthen segregation. It has done this through the federal urban renewal program, public housing and mortgage redlining.

# URBAN RENEWAL ("NEGRO REMOVAL") AND DISPLACEMENT

The Housing Act of 1949 enabled municipalities to use their power of eminent domain for "slum clearance," and the federal government provided funding to acquire property from existing owners and convey it to developers in accordance with a plan (Wright 1983, 232; Caro 1975, 777). While the policy was supposed to address unhealthy and unsafe conditions, the urban renewal projects were not required to house those who were displaced, nor was the new housing affordable to most original residents (Wright 1983, 226–227). Following eviction, black residents watched their neighborhoods get replaced not by better housing for them, but large-scale luxury development projects and highways (Meyer 2001, 55).

Opposition to urban renewal programs was a major part of the Civil Rights Movement, as urban renewal became widely known as "Negro removal." In New York City, supporters of racial justice fought to stop the displacement of one of the largest Latino neighborhoods in Manhattan, which was replaced by Lincoln Center. A legal challenge went all the way to the Supreme Court and led to a landmark ruling upholding the right of government to use eminent domain for urban redevelopment. Fierce battles broke out to prevent the displacement of minority communities in the West Side Urban Renewal Area, the Cooper Square Urban Renewal Area, and many other parts of the city.

# Opposition to urban renewal programs was a major part of the Civil Rights Movement, as urban renewal became widely known as "Negro removal."

At the same time as black neighborhoods were being uprooted to promote upscale development, many were also cleared to build urban sections of the Interstate Highway system, which drew federal resources away from the central cities and into the suburbs. City and state policymakers—and in New York City Robert Moses was the master—sought to harness federal highway dollars to assist in their reclamation of downtown real estate by condemning "slums" and routing highways directly through them. Highway projects in New York City alone displaced some 250,000 people (Mohl 2000, 227–234; Caro 1975, 19).

Although local authorities were required to provide adequate replacement housing in order to qualify for urban renewal funds, in practice this rarely happened (Massey and Denton 1993, 55). In the period 1949–1968, cities demolished 425,000 units of low-income housing and only built 125,000 new units, over half of which were luxury apartments (Wright 1981, 234). Only one-half of 1 percent of all planned federal expenditures in the period 1949–1964 was for relocation benefits (Gans 1962). New public housing projects were supposed to absorb the displaced, but these projects were routinely placed in existing poor and majority black neighborhoods, reinforcing segregation (Massey and Denton 1993, 56).

Federal funds for urban renewal, highway expansion, and many other federal projects required that they be used in accordance with local plans. Although the plans were reviewed by the federal government, local governments had significant autonomy. In practice, New York City determined the shape of new development.

# PUBLIC HOUSING: WAREHOUSING THE DISPLACED AND MINORITIES

Urban renewal did produce some low-income housing, starting with public housing. In the 1930s, the Public Works Administration (PWA) funded and carried out "slum clearance" programs and built new low-rent housing. Over its first four years, the PWA demolished 10,000 substandard units and developed 22,000 new ones. In 1935, the courts ruled that the federal government did not have the right to condemn private land for low-cost housing; so, the PWA set up state and local housing authorities to undertake the redevelopment and the construction of low-income housing. New York City was among the first municipalities to take advantage of the federal program.

Ultimately, this delegation of authority further entrenched racial divisions and local prejudices. PWA funding stipulated that housing projects would only house black people in neighborhoods that were already black, and if the neighborhood was mixed, new projects would house blacks and whites in the same proportions (Wright 1981, 225). The United States Housing Authority, created in 1937, went even further and tied "slum clearance" to new housing construction, which meant much of new public housing was built by displacing existing housing in black and low-income neighborhoods typically deemed slums.

On the surface, these policies appeared to ensure no net loss of housing, but they did far more for the building industry than for the poor and black communities who were displaced. The total supply of housing available to low-income working people did not increase even as the needs grew (Marcuse, 1986). In New York City's pioneering public housing projects built in 1937, for instance, many of the initial tenants were white, including construction workers and their families. In the throes of the Great Depression, public housing was as much a jobs program as a housing program. This changed after the Second World War. The Housing Act of 1949 and subsequent court rulings further expanded local powers of eminent domain, and public funding allowed cities to buy up even more "blighted" urban areas so they could now be given to private developers (Wright 1981, 232; Caro 1975, 777). The impact of these large-scale urban redevelopment projects was the massive displacement of black and other minority communities. In the end, urban renewal stimulated the building industry and displaced the poor and black communities that lived in its path.

# MORTGAGE AND INSURANCE REDLINING

The Federal Housing Administration (FHA), created in 1934, and its cousin, the 1944 G.I. Bill within the Veterans Administration (VA), expanded mortgages for homebuyers and provided a new, massive market for suburban development (Jackson 2008, 204–206). The FHA and VA programs favored single-family, owner-occupied housing types. Due to redlining, they were not available to many black homebuyers.

In 1933, the federal government created the Home Owners Loan Corporation (HOLC) to protect homeowners from foreclosure, which introduced the now ubiquitous long-term, self-amortizing mortgage that has enabled so many families to own their home. However, its methods of appraisal for lending led to systematic devaluation and denial of lending to neighborhoods with black populations through its now infamous practice of *redlining*. In assessing the desirability of neighborhoods, HOLC basically drew a red line around neighborhoods that were not considered desirable. One critical factor was whether more than five percent of the population was black. Banks usually did not offer loans to any homes within the red lines. They identified the presence of black residents as an indicator of decline, and presumed an inverse correlation between the concentration of black residents and the viability of investment. In some mostly-white neighborhoods, this spurred white flight to the suburbs, resulting in a neighborhood that became mostly black. HOLC appraisers generally classified all-black neighborhoods as "declined" without respect to the upkeep of the housing or surroundings, assuming that black populations both followed and caused declining property values (Jackson 2008, 202–203).

In the New York region, the discrepancy between urban and suburban FHA lending was stark. Between 1934 and 1960, FHA per capita lending for suburban Nassau was 11 times greater than in Brooklyn and 60 times greater than in the Bronx. The FHA effectively turned the building and insurance industries against the black and inner-city housing market, leading to the

**48**

redlining of entire cities and locking them into a spiral of decline (Jackson 2008, 211–213). A study of lending after World War II found that companies starkly decreased lending in urban areas over time: from 1945–1954 they did not issue any mortgages to 23 percent of urban census tracts; by 1966 they were not issuing mortgages to 67 percent of urban census tracts (Taylor 2014, 238–239).

In New York City, largely black neighborhoods such as Harlem and Bedford-Stuyvesant were redlined, depriving residents of access to the capital they needed to maintain their homes. White residents who were living in these neighborhoods could take advantage of the growing stock of affordable housing in the suburbs since race was not a barrier to them. Black residents, on the other hand, were excluded because of discriminatory practices in the sales and rental markets. City government failed to use its resources or considerable access to financial markets to promote redevelopment in these neighborhoods.

In New York City, largely black neighborhoods such as Harlem and Bedford-Stuyvesant were redlined, depriving residents of access to the capital they needed to maintain their homes.... City government failed to use its resources or considerable access to financial markets to promote redevelopment in these neighborhoods.

## 02.C Redlining in Manhattan.

*Many "redlined" neighborhoods remained segregated communities facing high poverty rates, such as Harlem and East Harlem. Other redlined areas faced redevelopment plans that displaced people of color, such as the Upper West Side.*

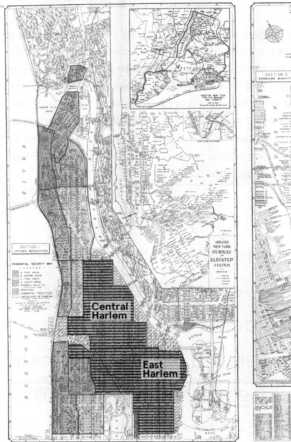

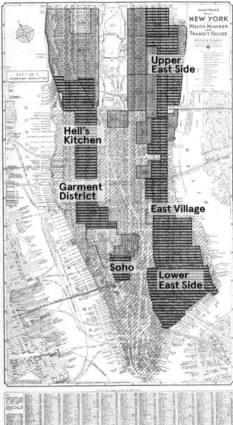

▤ Fourth Grade Residential Security
   (Redlined neighborhoods)

Hagstom's Home Owners Loan Coporation (HOLC) Map of New York House Number
and Transit Guide. Hagstrom Company, 1938.

White neighborhoods in all five boroughs qualified for support under federal mortgage programs; they also benefited from the sizeable tax deductions for mortgage interest — the single largest housing subsidy in the nation. In an effort to preserve its tax base, the city proved especially eager to sustain services and infrastructure in white neighborhoods, while it often wrote off minority neighborhoods, most notably during the fiscal crisis of the 1970s.

One of the most insidious results of redlining was that it reinforced the notion that black people cause urban decline, thus feeding racial exclusion. In fact, it was the banks, insurance companies, and federal and local governments that heavily contributed to decline as black residents struggled to maintain their homes and create businesses without access to capital and support from government. This contributed to white flight and later opened the door for predatory real estate brokers, investors, and lenders.

## HOUSING ABANDONMENT AND PLANNED SHRINKAGE

Even after the federal government and courts ended redlining, many local governments continued the practice of favoring expenditures in white neighborhoods while ignoring needs in black neighborhoods. This unequal treatment was on display in New York City during the fiscal crisis of the 1970s. When the city faced possible bankruptcy due to larger changes in global, national, and regional capital, severe budget cuts were made. Industry moved to the suburbs and around the world and the industrial labor force moved out of the city. Real estate capital fled large swaths of the city, resulting in widespread abandonment of housing in the South Bronx, Central Brooklyn, and Harlem, all communities of color. Banks, insurance companies, and landlords withdrew and the response of city government was to purposely withhold services in these neighborhoods. Roger Starr, the commissioner in charge of housing, famously called for "planned shrinkage" of the neighborhoods that were most seriously affected, essentially claiming that they had no right to exist. Services were withdrawn and vacant land and buildings were auctioned off instead of being redeveloped.

Planned shrinkage was understood in minority neighborhoods as a concept with deep racial undertones. The presumption was that once the cycle of decline had ended and the minority population left, the real estate market would move in and redevelop these areas. While thousands of buildings were abandoned, the people who stayed came together and organized, and were eventually able to press for housing programs that helped them to preserve their neighborhoods. These included programs created in the city's housing agency under the Division of Alternative Management Programs (DAMP).

While thousands of buildings were abandoned, the people who stayed came together and organized, and were eventually able to press for housing programs that helped them to preserve their neighborhoods.

## DISCRIMINATION IN HOUSING

After the 1968 Fair Housing Act, the city had clear authority to prosecute individual acts of discrimination in both private and public sectors, and over the years they have done so with limited resources. However, individual practices of discrimination continue and have impacts on entire neighborhoods while city government has done little to address the institutional elements in housing discrimination, some of which are mentioned below.

### BLOCKBUSTING AND RACIAL STEERING

In many white neighborhoods that are near black communities block-busting has been a common tool for using race to turn a quick profit. Blockbusters play on racial stereotypes and go door-to-door, and use advertising to warn white residents of the incoming "black invasion." White homeowners, fearing a precipitous decline in their home values, sell at below market value. The blockbuster then rents or sells the unit well above the market price to middle- and upper-class black families willing to pay more to live in better housing (Thabit 2003, 45). Because black loan applicants are disproportionately denied by banks, the realtor often acts as both seller and lender, charging high interest rates that lead incoming families to default and eviction. Some brokers illegally subdivide units and thus increase overcrowding as housing deteriorates. These practices further segregate black loan applicants across income levels. They can also

**52**

foster the myth that black people cause neighborhood decline (Massey and Denton 1993, 37–39).

Racial steering is perhaps the most common and durable form of housing discrimination. Real estate brokers use a host of informal methods to "steer" black people to black neighborhoods and keep them out of white neighborhoods. Federal and city funds support non-profit and legal aid groups that do "testing" for racial steering and advocate for people that experience housing discrimination. While there have been many individual cases resulting in legal challenges, the city has never moved beyond individual cases and undertaken a major campaign to change the way neighborhoods remain segregated through discriminatory practices by realtors and building owners.

**PREDATORY LENDING**

As more capital became available for investment in the real estate sector starting in the 1990s, lenders sought creative ways to open up new markets. Populations that had been redlined in the past were now targets for home mortgage loans. Predatory lending targets prospective and current homeowners by making loans under terms that lenders cannot afford to pay. Predatory loans are disproportionately marketed to poor neighborhoods and people of color. Victims of predatory lending may go into foreclosure, bankruptcy, or suffer other significant financial damage.[3] This practice was permitted by federal regulatory agencies and became widespread in the years leading up to the 2007–2008 financial crisis, when investment companies were bundling toxic loans in mortgage-backed securities.

In New York City, predatory practices were even more pervasive in the rental market. In a practice that tenant advocates dubbed "predatory equity," large financial institutions and real estate companies bought up occupied multi-family properties with the goal of removing rent-regulated tenants (using legal and illegal methods) and bringing in renters with higher incomes. The speculative investments were often based on inflated property values and rents. The market crash and tenant organizing threw a wrench into many of these plans, causing investors to default and leaving many people and buildings in distress. In both predatory lending and equity schemes, black and other minority communities were disproportionately represented among the victims.

**ANTI-DISCRIMINATION AND FAIR HOUSING LAWS**

In the 1960s, housing discrimination became a national issue and Congress passed legislation prohibiting racial discrimination in government-funded

## THE FAIR HOUSING ACT
## AND DEFINING DISCRIMINATION:
## INTENT VS. DISPARATE IMPACT

The Fair Housing Act prohibits discrimination based on race, gender, disability, religion and other protected classes. The law, though largely a response to intentional discrimination, does not require claims of fair housing violation to prove intent. Instead, it is sufficient to show that the action resulted in racial exclusion. In other words, if a housing program or policy has a disparate impact on racial groups or other protected classes, it is discriminatory. Disparate impact theory, while challenged, has been upheld by the courts and has guided case law for the past three decades.

In a 2015 ruling, Texas Department of Housing and Community Affairs et al. v. Inclusive Communities Project, Inc., et al, the United States Supreme Court affirmed that in order to prove racial discrimination it is sufficient to demonstrate a disparate impact of public policy without necessarily proving discriminatory intent.

housing. The law had limited impact, however, suffering from uneven enforcement. The law provided little recourse in local battles over the location of public housing projects, which were largely kept out of white, middle- and upper-income neighborhoods (Mohl 2000, 131, 195).

Following the historic Civil Rights Act of 1964, and following rebellions in central-city black neighborhoods, the Kerner Commission was convened by President Johnson to investigate the causes and propose remedies. The Commission declared discrimination and the exclusionary housing market a central cause. After decades of organizing by the Civil Rights Movement, President Johnson signed the Fair Housing Act of 1968 (Civil Rights Act Title VIII), which prohibited the denial of housing based on race. Lower courts have since used the law to block racial steering, race-based appraisal practices, redlining, exclusionary zoning and planning, public housing site selection and demolition, and discriminatory community development activities. However, the Fair Housing Act has been hampered by persistently weak enforcement and subsequent court decisions have limited efforts by the Civil Rights Movement to use the courts to address discrimination (Meyer 2001, 207, 216).

# THE RISE AND TRIUMPH OF "AFFORDABLE HOUSING"

Since the fiscal crisis of the 1970s, government at all levels has disinvested in public housing and turned away from direct subsidies of new and existing housing. Instead, government has subsidized financial investors and private developers through public-private partnerships. The underlying assumption for this shift is that public housing is the problem and private housing—the private market—is the solution. Conservatives in Congress fought public housing from the beginning, and when they couldn't stop it they cut funds needed to maintain the quality of housing; then they blamed deteriorating conditions in public housing on the program itself. When Ronald Reagan became president in 1980, he definitively marked the shift away from direct public funding, and every administration since then has followed the same path. The new solution to housing problems would be to provide tax incentives, regulatory relief, and subsidies to the private sector, so that the new housing would "trickle-down" to low-income people. The Low-Income Housing Tax Credit program, now the largest source of subsidies for new low-income housing, is a boon to private investors and results in housing built in segregated neighborhoods.

Another major criticism of public housing is that it concentrates and isolates poor people, which is presumed (without clear evidence) to increase crime and the "culture of poverty."[4] The new approach instead encouraged mixed-income development, creating opportunities for low-income people to move into better neighborhoods (now known as "moving to opportunity") where schools and other services are presumably better and chances of moving out of poverty are improved. Many long-time liberal supporters of public housing have embraced this new approach as a solution to racial segregation, since government funds would be used to integrate neighborhoods.

Until now, New York City has been a prominent exception to the decline in public housing. It has managed to maintain the country's largest public housing stock without any major demolition or privatization (Dagen Bloom 2008). This is not only due to a history of relatively good management, but also has been abetted by operating and capital subsidies from government and support from portions of the business community. This is changing rapidly, however, as the impact of federal cutbacks in capital and operating subsidies grows and city and state support evaporates. A heated real estate industry is increasingly coveting centrally located public housing sites. In Mayor Michael Bloomberg's last year in office, the administration presented a proposal to build market-rate housing on eight public housing sites in choice Manhattan locations (Angotti and Morse 2014). Facing opposition by public housing tenants, the mayor withdrew his proposal. However, Mayor Bill de Blasio's recent proposal to "save public housing" has resurrected the idea and expanded it into an elaborate long-term strategy to turn public housing into a public–private enterprise in which the private sector retains the most valuable assets and dominates future decision-making (City of New York 2015).

In the last chapter we will return to the question of public housing and make a case that a return to full public financing of housing for those who need it the most would be a major step towards economic and racial equality in New York City.

## THE PUBLIC-PRIVATE PARTNERSHIP

Beyond public housing, the public–private partnership has been New York City's preferred option for the provision of housing over the last four decades. After the fiscal crisis, private housing and commercial development, not direct public subsidies, were promoted as the antidote to widespread disinvestment and abandonment. Thus were born the 421-a and J-51 tax incentives, bond financing and liberal zoning measures that have made real estate development in New York City a most profitable enterprise. The housing boom that these measures helped to create have led, since the 1980s to large increases in land values and rents, the displacement of many low-income minorities, and the creation of massive homelessness.

Coinciding with the decline of public support for low-income housing there has been a parallel rise of what we know today as "affordable housing." Affordable housing has become a euphemism for "middle-class housing." This is more politically acceptable to those who oppose any form of low-income housing. Affordable housing programs since the fiscal crisis have used public funds to finance new construction and the rehabilitation of existing housing units. Mayor Ed Koch (1978–1989) implemented an ambitious housing program, which included public financing for one to three family homes for middle-income homebuyers. In his 12 years as mayor, Michael Bloomberg managed to complete around 175,000 affordable housing units, most of which served middle-income households. The program successfully preserved over 100,000 existing affordable units, but also spurred new development targeted to moderate incomes,[5] which helped fuel displacement in gentrifying neighborhoods. Mayor de Blasio's 10-year housing plan calls for 200,000 affordable housing units and relies

**56**

on public-private partnerships that could very well have a similar impact on neighborhoods.

Mayor Michael Bloomberg managed to complete around 175,000 affordable housing units, most of which served middle-income households. The program successfully preserved over 100,000 existing affordable units, but also spurred new development targeted to moderate incomes, which helped fuel displacement in gentrifying neighborhoods.

The main problem with these affordable housing programs is that the units being preserved or built are not affordable to people living in the neighborhoods where they are located. This is illustrated in the Williamsburg and Harlem cases discussed in the following chapters. In neighborhoods with low-income minority populations where land values and rents are rising, these programs contribute to displacement of those who need housing the most and cannot afford to pay higher housing costs. This result is assured when the Area Median Income (AMI) is used as a benchmark for eligibility for the new housing units. The AMI is calculated by HUD based on incomes for the city and a portion of the suburbs. Typically the AMI is four to five times higher than the median income in low-income neighborhoods, which excludes the majority of existing residents from eligibility for new units. Units are allocated according to a lottery that often excludes large numbers of low-income people of color. There is a racial edge to the lotteries since preference is given to those with excellent credit ratings (discriminatory and predatory practices make it difficult for people of color to maintain one) and, due to stop-and-frisk practices and the mass incarceration of blacks and Latinos, many are unable to qualify because they have been arrested at some point in their lives.

Another problem with most of the affordable housing is that guarantees of affordability are not permanent. In some programs requirements that occupants fall below maximum income limits expire in only a few years, and government is often unable to monitor compliance.[6] Thus, over decades New York City's investment of billions of dollars on affordable housing have basically subsidized real estate speculation. And government has never undertaken a study to determine whether these programs have contributed to the displacement of low-income minority communities.

Many residents in communities now facing upzoning perceive affordable housing as the fig leaf that will ease the way for widespread development and displacement. Promises that a rezoning will bring new affordable housing are intended to quell fears that new market-rate development will displace low-income people, yet too many people have seen the results of past affordable housing promises. As we argue elsewhere, it is clear that many existing affordable units are lost when speculators and landlords anticipate an upzoning. Too often more affordable units are lost than gained, and since it usually takes many years to develop affordable housing, by the time it is completed it is no longer of use to those who have already been displaced.

# INCLUSIONARY ZONING

After years of advocacy by community-based organizations, and facing increasing opposition to rezonings, the Bloomberg administration adopted inclusionary zoning in some of its rezoning proposals. Inclusionary zoning provided a 20 percent bonus in floor area to developers who provided 20 percent of units as affordable housing (using the HUD AMI). This was instituted as a voluntary measure. After a decade in practice, however, this measure produced relatively few new "affordable" units.

The de Blasio administration has made inclusionary housing mandatory in all upzonings. The new measure allows a certain amount of flexibility so the developer can choose from among several basic formulas. While mandatory inclusionary zoning is known to have been effective in other cities, it still would not apply everywhere in New York City, only in areas with major new development. It would still use the AMI as a bench-mark. And at the end of the day, up to 80 percent of the new housing units created would be market-rate, which in practice means luxury housing, which in turn leads to rising land values and rents and has a ripple effect on the surrounding area. In low-income communities of color this is likely to result in substantial displacement.

And at the end of the day, up to 80 percent of the new housing units created would be market-rate, which in practice means luxury housing, which in turn leads to rising land values and rents and has a ripple effect on the surrounding area. In low-income communities of color this is likely to result in substantial displacement.

## DISPLACEMENT AND RACE

In sum, New York City's zoning and housing policies combine to reinforce the market-driven process of displacement of low-income communities of color. The case studies that follow give specific examples of how these policies play out in New York City neighborhoods.

The first change needed is for the city to recognize that displacement is a problem and that race and income play a major role in determining who gets displaced and the options available to them. New York City does not attempt to measure displacement resulting from its zoning and housing policies, yet this would have to be the first step in constructing alternative policies. Extensive community-based planning in every neighborhood, especially those that are under pressure from new development, would allow communities to work with government to comprehensively plan for the future. This would allow neighborhoods and city government to work together to understand displacement pressures and the effects of public policy on low-income people of color, and to develop equitable long-term solutions. We will return to community-based planning in the last chapter.

**Endnotes**

1. Daisy Gonzalez and Katie Lyon-Hart provided research assistance for this chapter.

2. This is a largely Orthodox Jewish neighborhood.

3. See https://comptroller.nyc.gov/general-information/predatory-lending.

4. This has been a continuing debate among social scientists and it is beyond the scope here to fully argue the matter. We are convinced by the notion that concentrated poverty is not the major problem. The major problem is poverty and inequality. The notion of concentrated poverty began with the early 20th-century progressive reformers and was boosted by the "culture of poverty" theory popularized by Oscar Lewis in the 1970s, and "spatial de-concentration" became a rallying cry of many housing and planning experts. Many factors contribute to poverty, including access to education, services, and employment, and racial discrimination. There is some evidence that when poor people move to mixed-income neighborhoods their lives improve, but there is no evidence that scattering poor people across the land, by itself, makes them any less poor. People living in low-density and rural areas experience poverty no less acutely than those living in densely developed urban areas (See Angotti 1993, 13–15).

5. According to a December 21, 2013 press release from the Office of the Mayor.

6. See http://www.anhd.org/wp-content/uploads/2011/07/Real-Affordability-Evaluation-of-the-Bloomberg-Housing-Program2.pdf;

   Good Place to Work, Hard Place to Live, Closing the Door 2013—CSS http://b.3cdn.net/nycss/1c9817fd6343bf9c88_lkm6va7t8.pdf.

# CHAPTER THREE

# WILLIAMSBURG: ZONING OUT LATINOS

**PHILIP DEPAOLO AND SYLVIA MORSE**

This is the story of how the Greenpoint and Williamsburg communities labored for more than a decade to produce a plan to guide their long-term future, only to be excluded from the city's top-down zoning process that dramatically gentrified the neighborhoods. The city approved the community plans in name only, launching its own rezoning that sparked luxury high-rise development displacing residents and businesses—the exact outcome the community plans rejected. This is a story of how New York City undermines democratic community-based planning by zoning without a plan.

Following decades of neglect by city government, residents engaged in a community-based planning process beginning in the late 1980s to address environmental injustice, the need for affordable housing, and preservation of industrial businesses and jobs. Two plans, the Williamsburg and Greenpoint community plans, were officially approved in 2002 by the CPC. Perhaps the most important element in the plans, reflecting a broad consensus in these diverse neighborhoods, was that development along the waterfront reflect the historic low-rise character of the neighborhood and preserve the mixture of industry and housing.

However, the 2005 Williamsburg-Greenpoint rezoning plan, initiated by the city, led to the development of high-rise luxury housing on the waterfront and throughout the neighborhoods, spurring dramatic increases in housing costs and residential displacement. The city's rezoning supported

**03.A Mural in Los Sures, Also Known as the Southside, a Longstanding Puerto Rican Community in Williamsburg.**

*Photo: Tom Angotti, 2016.*

Zoned Out!

land speculation and unaffordable housing by allowing large-scale residential development on the industrial waterfront, and in mixed-use areas of Williamsburg and Greenpoint. Low-income residents, many of whom were Latino, struggled to stay as rents rose and landlords undermined rent protections. Industry left and more jobs were lost. What began as a gradual neighborhood improvement process before the rezoning, in which most homeowners and renters were able to survive, ended in a massive displacement of industry, residents, and the small, locally owned businesses that served them.

Since the rezoning, Williamsburg and Greenpoint have become predominantly white, even as the white population declines citywide. The rezoned area saw the most dramatic increase in the white population. The 2005 rezoning also enhanced segregation, with the remaining low-income minority populations isolated in small pockets. Subsequent rezonings and other policy changes have failed to address, and instead enhanced, rising housing costs and displacement.

## 03.B Neighborhood Map:
## Greenpoint and Williamsburg–Brooklyn Community District 1

# BACKGROUND

For more than a century Williamsburg and Greenpoint, located in North Brooklyn, were immigrant, working-class neighborhoods with a rich mixture of industry and housing. Much of the area was developed in the early 20th century after the Williamsburg Bridge opened in 1903. What evolved was a series of low-rise residential communities adjacent to industry, where many residents walked to work.

Southern Italian immigrants settled on Williamsburg's northside, a Hasidic community grew on the south side, and a Polish community settled in Greenpoint. The Brooklyn Navy Yard, a major employer along the waterfront, closed after World War II, and when most of the Port of New York moved to New Jersey soon after that, many maritime industries shut down. Still, the neighborhood retained a large number of smaller industries and a few large ones, like the Domino Sugar factory. As a result of city disinvestment and white flight in the post-war period, Latino—primarily Puerto Rican, and later, Dominican— communities expanded on the south and east side of Williamsburg. There has been a long history of tension and conflict, as well as cooperation, between these Latino and white communities, particularly related to new housing development, segregation, environmental justice, affordability, and displacement.

One battleground for racial conflict and cooperation has been the struggle over environmental quality. During the 1970s fiscal crisis, Williamsburg and Greenpoint lost thousands of industrial jobs, and with them, residents—most of them white. City officials saw vacant industrial land in this working-class community as "underutilized" and allowed the siting of large waste facilities with minimal regulation. Absent a strong political and tax base, the working-class residents, many of them people of color, fought as part of a citywide coalition of environmental justice groups for a more equitable and sustainable waste management plan.

The city's policy of reducing services during the fiscal crisis created opportunities for real estate speculation. Beginning in the late 1970s, Williamsburg offered artists an inexpensive alternative to gentrifying lower Manhattan, and produced new lofts, studios, galleries, shops, and networking spaces. As the city's economy rebounded in the 1990s and 2000s, Williamsburg saw an influx of speculative real estate capital. Incomes remained relatively stagnant, however, rising 10 percent over 10 years, while median rents rose 34 percent. At the same time, industry continued to decline; between 1991 and 2002, Community District 1 lost 40 percent of its industrial jobs and more than 60 percent of its manufacturing jobs.[1] With a shrinking industrial base and growing residential

**64**

# HOUSING DISCRIMINATION IN WILLIAMSBURG

In areas with high concentrations of Latino residents,
particularly on the south side, the majority of residents
are renters and many are low-income. Many are vulnerable to
real estate speculation, which has sparked racial tensions.
Another trigger of racial conflict has been discrimination in
tenant selection for public housing and city-backed affordable
housing development.

### Discrimination by the Public Housing Authority
A state court found that the New York City Housing Authority
had discriminated against non-white tenants, many of them
Puerto Rican, for placement in three housing developments in
parts of Williamsburg where white populations, including the
Hasidic Jewish community, were growing.

*Williamsburg Fair Housing Committee v.New York City Housing
Authority, 76 Civ. 2125.*http://www.newyorklawjournal.
com/id=1202504189597/Williamsburg-Fair-Housing-
Committee-v-New-York-City-Housing-Authority-76-Civ-
2125?slreturn=20150413004701.

### Discrimination in Affordable Housing
A community coalition challenged a city-backed proposed
affordable housing development known as Broadway Triangle,
being developed by a non-profit organization based in
the Hasidic Jewish community of South Williamsburg, as
discriminatory against black and Latino residents. Plaintiffs
argued that the city failed to analyze the potential racial
impacts of the plan, and that tenant selection policy favored
white residents by offering local preference to Williamsburg
rather than the adjacent, predominantly black and Latino
Bedford-Stuyvesant area (based on Community District
boundaries). The State Supreme Court granted plaintiff's
request for a preliminary injunction in 2012, and the project
has remained in legal and political limbo.

*Broadway Triangle Community Coalition v. Michael Bloomberg,
State Supreme Court, New York County, Index No. 112799/09*
http://www.nyclu.org/files/releases/Broadway_Injunction_
Decision_1.4.12.pdf

**03.C Typical low-rise housing in Williamsburg.**

Photo: Tom Angotti, 2016

market, many landlords began to convert industrial properties for residential use, often illegally. Low-income and working-class people thus faced a shortage of living wage local jobs and rising housing costs (Susser and Stabrowski 2015).

Facing intense economic pressures and displacement, residents organized to address Greenpoint and Williamsburg's housing and economic needs. Building on years of grassroots environmental justice organizing, residents and activists set out to create a plan for their neighborhood. In 2002, the city officially adopted community-based plans (known as 197-a plans)[2] for Williamsburg and Greenpoint. The plans recommended increasing the availability of low-rise affordable housing, improving access to open space and the waterfront, promoting non-polluting industry, and reducing the concentration of noxious waste facilities.

If there was one common principle that was widely shared by residents and businesses who participated in the planning process it was that new development, particularly along the portions of the waterfront that were undeveloped, should be in keeping with the low- to mid-rise character of the neighborhood. The overwhelming consensus was that the community did not want luxury high-rise towers on the waterfront. The plans sent a clear message that the mixture of small industry and commerce and housing was a positive element to be preserved. In hundreds of community

**66**

meetings people from all ethnic groups and income levels set aside their differences to reach this consensus.

Just a few years later, however, the city launched its own rezoning plan. In May 2005, the city approved a comprehensive rezoning of the Greenpoint-Williamsburg waterfront to promote high-density residential development.

# THE 2005 WILLIAMSBURG REZONING

Once the ink dried on the officially approved community plan, the Department of City Planning (DCP) began its own study of the community. However, this was not a comprehensive and exhaustive study that considered the community in all its complexity and diversity, its problems and opportunities, its history and future. It was a rezoning study, which began by looking at floor area ratios, "underutilized" land parcels, and opportunities for new development. It was not as comprehensive as the community plan and did not take into consideration the broad and negative impacts the rezoning would have on existing affordable housing, low-income people, and racial minorities. It took no more than two years for DCP to put together its rezoning plan, run it through the requisite Uniform Land Use Review Procedure, and get it approved by the city council in 2005.[3]

The proposed rezoning targeted approximately 200 blocks of north Williamsburg and parts of Greenpoint for new residential development. DCPs stated intention was to "facilitate housing and open spaces, and light industry and commercial uses" in both "established residential communities as well as adjoining areas that have been mostly vacant and derelict for years," along a two-mile-long waterfront and in surrounding parts of the neighborhoods.[4] DCP stated that the rezoning would address the community's goals for affordable housing and maintain the neighborhood character, as laid out in the community's 197-a plan.

There were three major elements to the rezonings: residential uses were permitted in formerly industrial areas, buildings with significantly larger height and bulk were allowed, particularly on the waterfront, and new "mixed-use" zones were introduced, which permitted either industrial or residential uses in formerly industrial zones. The rezoning included blocks that were at or near the epicenter of Williamsburg's growth and high-end real estate speculation. The plan allowed for nearly 55 million square feet of residential development within those blocks alone, a staggering 298 percent increase from the existing allowable 13.7 million square feet.

The plan faced significant local opposition and criticism from planning experts and neighborhood advocates (Ferguson 2005). Many residents

## 03.D Greenpoint–Williamsburg Rezoning, 2005.

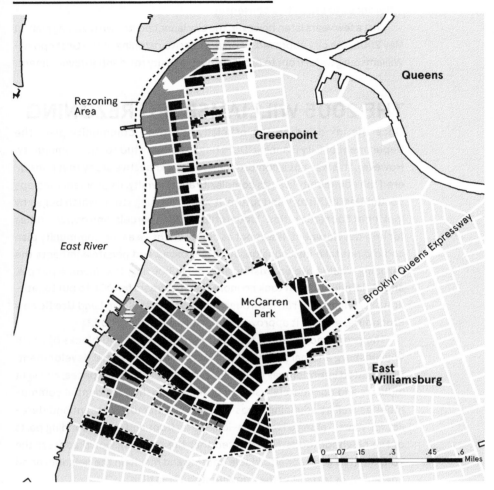

Rezoning Area

Queens

Greenpoint

East River

Brooklyn Queens Expressway

McCarren Park

East Williamsburg

0  .07  .15     .3        .45      .6
Miles

■ Upzoned Residential

▓ Upzoned Mixed
Manufacturing/Residential

≡ Manufacturing zoning preserved

New York City Department of City Planning, December 2015.

and community representatives first questioned the plan's impact on local manufacturing. The new mixed-use districts, which allowed for light
manufacturing, commercial, and residential uses, were criticized as tools
for converting industrial facilities to residential. Rents are highest for residential uses in the current market, reflecting higher land values. Greater
height and bulk capacity for residential buildings yields a larger number
of rental or ownership units and thus a larger rent roll or higher sales for
each project. Landowners of industrial properties thus had tremendous
incentive to convert them to residential use, or sell them to speculators
who would do it. Most likely many property transfers occurred well in advance of the final approval of the rezoning. Those industrial businesses that
did remain in the area would be challenged to hold onto their properties
or identify new locations (Angotti 2005).

The city ignored the concerns of residents and business owners. At the
same time, a citywide study found that "some landlords in industrial areas
were reluctant to offer long-term leases to their [industrial] tenants [and
were] keeping real estate vacant, or offering it only on a short term basis,
in the hopes that a residential rezoning or conversion in the future would
[raise] property values," *Curbed* reported (Rosenberg, 2014). DCP, however, went forward with its mixed-use districts. Businesses that would be
directly displaced by the plan, such as Bayside Fuel, as well as those who
feared indirect displacement, opposed and critiqued the plan.

As reported by Sarah Ferguson (2005), long-time Williamsburg
manufacturing business owner Stephanie Eisenberg put it succinctly:
"Businesses like ours can't survive with that kind of real estate pressure.
Once the property values rise, we'll have no choice but to sell out." Some
of this business displacement occurred when the rezoning plans were first
announced, as local business owner Nevett Steele told Ferguson: "It's already forcing people out in a panic. Landlords are trying to get rid of people right away in anticipation. They're already jacking up the rents."

The loss of industry in the Greenpoint-Williamsburg area was recognized in the community's 197-a plan, but the plan insisted that an extensive and participatory community process would be required to determine
specific planning and redevelopment goals and tools to address industry
loss. The DCP, however, determined unilaterally that it would use zoning
to create what it called a mixed-use district that nevertheless allowed for
dense, speculative residential development. Sarah Ferguson noted:

> Under the guise of responding to the community's demand to redevelop the
> waterfront, the Bloomberg administration is pushing a rezoning plan far more
> radical than residents ever asked for (Ferguson 2005).

Another serious problem with the city's rezoning plan was its lack of sufficient provision for affordable housing. In response to the Environmental Impact Statement submitted with the rezoning proposal, many residents and advocacy groups commented on the need for affordable housing and the insufficient provisions in the plan. Local resident coalitions and affordable housing advocates, citing successful financial models, submitted public comment calling for a requirement that 40 percent of new residential units be affordable. Property owners on the waterfront and real estate interests, on the other hand, spoke in favor of the plan. Echoing developer comments, DCP dismissed calls for mandatory inclusionary housing programs as infeasible and counterproductive, ignoring established programs in other large US cities.[5]

Concerns regarding housing affordability focused on the potential displacement of low- and moderate-income renters, particularly Latinos. DCP "project[ed] the resultant displacement of some 2,500 existing residents to make room for the newcomers," while housing advocates "suggest[ed] that between 7,500–10,000 families [would] ultimately be displaced unless almost half of the new units [were] required to be truly affordable."[6]

In response to community advocacy, the rezoning ultimately offered some pathways to affordable housing development and preservation. The

## HOW SPECULATION INDUCED BY REZONING AFFECTED ONE BUILDING

According to a report from Rutgers University, "184 Kent is a landmark building that exemplifies gentrification and price speculation related to rezoning. The model industrial site containing many important features made specifically for industrial firms was pitted against the windfall of profits available to the building's owner if he redeveloped it to enter the residential market. The building had illegal residential lofts for an unknown period of time, and went for an official variance in 2000 to develop units with rents well beyond the reach of most low- and moderate-income residents."

Source: Kathe Newman, et. al, *Gentrification and Rezoning: Williamsburg-Greenpoint*, Community Development Studio, Rutgers University, Spring 2007,http://rwv.rutgers.edu/wp-content/uploads/2013/08/2007_SPRING_CD_Studio_Presentation_Text.pdf.

rezoning included voluntary incentives for developers of large market-rate developments to include a portion of affordable units.[7] The city promised that subsidies, tax incentives, and non-profit partnerships would produce 3,548 affordable housing units. Recognizing testimony from residents, and housing and legal aid groups that complained of landlord harassment, illegal rent increases and evictions of low-income residents, most of them people of color, the city later adopted an Anti-Harassment Zone and included a $2 million legal fund for tenants. These programs, however, were too little and too late; they would largely fail to address the enormous needs and prevent significant displacement. Income-targeted housing units identify target populations earning less than a given percentage of the city's Area Median Income, but in Williamsburg that percentage was much higher (Susser and Stabrowski 2015).

Residents and advocacy groups were also concerned that new commercial uses and investments in public open space would lead to expanded inequalities. The officially approved Williamsburg 197-a plan recommended that new public space be developed on the waterfront. However, this assumed that there would be contextual development and affordable housing on and near the waterfront. In public testimony, residents expressed the fear that:

> Relying on the developers to build the esplanade... could end up like the so-called Gold Coast in Jersey City, where the waterfront is technically "open" to the general public, but in reality isn't all that inviting (Ferguson 2015).

**03.E Typical waterfront residential development in Williamsburg.**

*Photo: Tom Angotti, 2016.*

Today, new towers wall off the waterfront open space from the surrounding community. While formally open to the public, much of the open space functions as a back yard for residents and accessory space for businesses serving a largely upscale new population.

## FLAWED PARTICIPATION PROCESS, UNEQUAL OUTCOMES

There were many public meetings about the rezoning, but they were held after the zoning proposal was prepared by DCP. The initial proposal was developed without the meaningful involvement of residents or community organizations and did not substantially build on the findings of the 197-a plan. The meetings with DCP were more theater than substance, and there was no genuine involvement in the decision-making process.

The city held required public outreach meetings, primarily through the local community board, to present the plan and receive public comment. Large numbers of residents organized and demanded to be heard at these meetings. For example, a November 2004 DCP hearing drew 1,500 residents. However, when residents found that these meetings did not allow for any serious participation, "they stormed out of the meeting and in four languages said they didn't want to lose their neighborhood," according to community organizer Beka Economopoulos. "So we brought together a number of local arts activists and tried to help show the strength of the community [197-a] plan" (Hamm 2005).

From the beginning, residents were particularly concerned about the racial impacts of the plan. Contextual rezoning offered some protection against speculative redevelopment in predominantly white sections of Williamsburg with higher rates of homeownership. However, it left the Latino community, predominantly renters with lower average income than white Williamsburg residents, without any protections from unscrupulous landlords and speculators. Language barriers and insufficient outreach by the city limited the opportunities for full involvement by the Latino community.

From the beginning, residents were particularly concerned about the racial impacts of the plan.

**72**

One resident activist told reporters: "We will not become another luxury enclave like Battery Park City. We will not let them take away our diversity" (Ferguson 2005). A public comment on the Environmental Impact Statement argued that: "The plan will ruin the existing mix of races and incomes and uses in Greenpoint-Williamsburg, which is what makes the community great."[8]

The plan was ultimately approved by the City Planning Commission (CPC) and City Council. The final insult to public participation was the inclusion of last-minute amendments based on closed-door discussions at the City Council, after the public review process had been completed. The Chair of the City Council Land Use Committee Melinda Katz stated that, "a lot of these agreements were made very late last night or early this morning" (Keller, 2005).

Behind-the-scenes negotiations conducted by the mayor's office also led to a 30-page memorandum from city hall that promised a series of community benefits. These negotiations gave the appearance of cooperation and flexibility on the part of the administration but in fact led to a long list of empty promises. A decade later, with a new administration in place, it is clear that memos such as this one are unenforceable and only help to legitimize public actions that face enormous local opposition.

# THE IMPACT OF THE REZONING

In the ten years since the rezoning, Williamsburg and Greenpoint were transformed by high-rise luxury condominiums, high-end hotels, new upscale restaurant and commercial uses, rising rents, and a population boom that is straining local services and infrastructure. These changes had a dramatic effect on Williamsburg's population, particularly low- and moderate-income minorities.

While advocates of the development use these changes as evidence of success, large numbers of Williamsburg residents and businesses were forced to move because of rising prices and rents. Income levels in Williamsburg are rising, mostly because of the higher-income newcomers. For Latino residents, incomes did not rise. In addition, the Latino population is rapidly shrinking. Low-income residents are being displaced while higher income, predominantly white residents move in to pay higher rents or buy new, high-priced condominium units.

**03.F  Marketing real estate in Williamsburg.**

*Photo: Tom Angotti, 2016.*

# NEW UPSCALE RESIDENTIAL DEVELOPMENT AND LOSS OF AFFORDABLE HOUSING

New residential development facilitated by the rezoning targets upper-income, small households, leaving aside the low- and moderate-income Latinos who tend to have larger families and require larger units. New homeownership opportunities and luxury rents were out of their reach.

Top local and global developers targeted the rezoned area for new massive luxury condominiums and rental complexes. The glass towers along the waterfront tout luxury amenities and views of Manhattan and charge rents upwards of $2,200 for a studio apartment, some reaching nearly $10,000 per month (Gregor 2014).

Backers of the rezoning claimed that an increase in the housing supply would reduce rents and house prices. The housing stock grew 23 percent between 2000 and 2010 but this coincided with increasing rents and home values. In the area that was rezoned, residential and commercial property values increased nearly 250 percent between 2002 and 2013, and median monthly gross rents swelled from $949 to $1,603 (Goldberg 2015, 51). Furthermore, the bulk of new housing has been in units for sale rather than rentals, thousands of which remain vacant (Furman Center 2014).[9]

**74**

The city claimed that the rezoning would produce 3,548 new affordable units, facilitated by subsidy programs, non-profit community partners, and the disposition of city-owned land. The 2005 "Greenpoint-Williamsburg Inclusionary Housing Program" included a combination of voluntary floor area bonuses and tax benefits for developers that promised to produce low- and middle-income affordable units. The 421-a tax abatement program promised to increase housing affordability by incentivizing the production of income-targeted units in luxury developments. In the rezoned waterfront area, the 421-a program required that recipients of the tax benefit set aside at least 20 percent of a development as rent regulated, income-targeted units. In the upland areas, the city offered tax relief to any new multi-family construction on blighted, vacant, or underutilized properties (City of New York 2005).

While the market-rate housing shot up virtually overnight, *most of the affordable units that were promised have yet to materialize*. As of 2013 only 19 of the 1,345 affordable housing units that were to be built on city owned land were developed (Hoffman 2013). The city pledged that one-third of the new housing units developed in the rezoned area would be affordable, but, according to a January 2016 report, only 16 percent of the more than 9,000 new housing units built were income-targeted (Reynoso 2016).[10] A new large-scale mixed-use development, Greenpoint Landing, is slated to bring approximately 1,400 income-targeted units to the area; 91 affordable units have been created to date. The city has not released updated figures on the total number of affordable units produced or preserved in the rezoned area (Anuta 2015; Plitt 2015).

The rezoning also failed to *preserve* affordable housing. According to tenant advocates, the harassment, overcharging, and eviction of low- and moderate-income tenants of rent-regulated housing has persisted since the rezoning (Susser and Stabrowski 2005). In 2011, the most recent year for which data is available, rent-stabilized and subsidized housing (excluding public housing) accounted for 51.7 percent of Greenpoint-Williamsburg's housing stock, down from 64 percent at the time of the rezoning (Furman Center 2005; 2013).

# DISPLACEMENT OF THE LATINO POPULATION

Between 2000 and 2013, the population of the Greenpoint-Williamsburg rezoning area grew by 18 percent, compared to a 2 percent growth rate for Brooklyn and 3 percent city wide. This growth was not uniform; Latino

**03.G Changes in Rent in Greenpoint-Williamsburg, 2000-2013.**

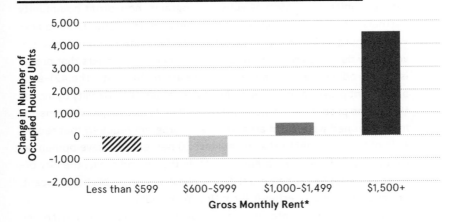

*Gross rent is the monthly contract rent plus monthly utilities.

U.S. Census Bureau, American Community Survey, 2014.

residents were displaced while the newcomers were mostly white. The white population in the rezoning area increased by 73 percent, compared to a 2 percent decline citywide. The Hispanic/Latino population declined by 18 percent, compared to a 10 percent increase citywide (Goldberg 2015). Among Latinos, according to the 2010 US Census, the historically prevalent Dominican and Puerto Rican population has declined the most.

The white population in the rezoning area increased by 73 percent, compared to a 2 percent decline citywide. The Hispanic/Latino population declined by 18 percent, compared to a 10 percent increase citywide.

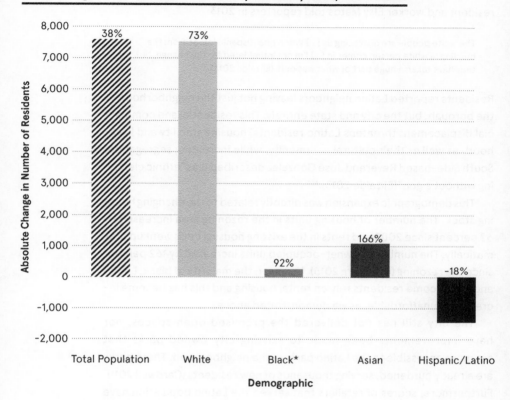

*The growth rate of black residents in the rezoning area is due to the small number of black residents who lived within the rezoning area before 2005; the increase in the number of black residents, 250, is extremely small relative to the number of white residents who moved into the area, 7, 505.

Leo Goldberg, based on U.S. Census Bureau, American Community Survey 2013 data.

What the numbers show, residents know intuitively. As Williamsburg resident and worker Elsy Matos told reporters in 2013:

> The white people are displacing us [...] When one Hispanic leaves from the building, a white person comes in [...] I'm not intimidated for the change, but they have taken a huge part of what was ours (Elizalde 2013).[11]

Residents reported Latino neighbors leaving not just the neighborhood or the borough, but the city and state entirely. This residential and commercial displacement threatens Latino residents' housing stability and livelihood, as well as their cultural community, while increasing segregation. South Side-based Reverend José Gonzalez described it as "ethnic cleansing without a gun"(Elizalde 2013).[12]

This demographic expansion was directly related to the changing housing stock. The number of housing units in the rezoning area increased by 62 percent since 2005 and rents in the existing housing units went up dramatically. The number of owner-occupied units increased by 162 percent since the rezoning (Goldberg 2015). However, the majority of black, Latino and low-income residents rely on rental housing and this has become increasingly unaffordable, as we demonstrated above.

The city still has not delivered the promised open spaces, nor have improvements been made to existing city-owned parks that are more accessible to the Latino parts of the neighborhood. These parks are already burdened, serving thousands of new residents (Cardwell 2011). Furthermore, scores of retailers that served the Latino population have been shuttered and replaced by restaurants, bars, and boutiques serving higher-income populations. Very few Latino-owned businesses remain.

# THE LOSS OF INDUSTRY

One of the stated purposes of the rezoning was to preserve and expand light manufacturing. However, the new mixed-use zones offer no substantial protections for manufacturing businesses, which are being displaced by residential uses that can afford higher rents. As a result, the rezoned area has lost nearly 8 million square feet of manufacturing uses, while gaining 12 million square feet of housing (Goldberg 2014, 51). Some new manufacturing businesses have come to the area, though these tend to be smaller, boutique companies with fewer employees than their predecessors, and do not necessarily hire locally.

Incentive programs for businesses outlined in the rezoning failed to produce meaningful results. An Industrial Business Zone (IBZ) created with the goal of preserving industrial uses had limited success. Businesses still could not combat rising commercial rents. For example, one business owner located in the IBZ reported that his landlord insisted on raising his monthly rent from $7,400 to more than $16,000, knowing it would result in his eviction (Rosenberg 2014). Other uses such as transient hotels, nightclubs, and restaurants yield much higher monthly rents than manufacturing. As of spring 2014, the Greenpoint-Williamsburg IBZ saw the development of three hotels, with an additional nine in the planning stages (Pasquarelli 2015). According to *Curbed.com*, industrial employment in the Greenpoint-Williamsburg waterfront area dropped from around 7,500 jobs in 2000 to 3,600 in 2009. Moreover, the organizations that support industrial businesses have lost vital city funding and reduced assistance to struggling businesses. As reported in *Curbed*:

> Funding for the organizations that support manufacturing around the city has declined ... The East Williamsburg Valley Industrial Development Company (EWVIDCO), for example, which manages two IBZs in North Brooklyn [...] has seen its budget from the city cut in half in just a few years; funding has dropped from $320,000 in 2010 to just under $160,000 last year, according Leah Archibald, the executive director of the organization. Many industrial advocates once again feel that the former mayor—as well as the DCP under Bloomberg-appointed director Amanda Burden—never really took the industries they represented seriously (Rosenberg 2014).

By eliminating manufacturing zones, the only protection against displacement due to residential development, the 2005 rezoning doomed industrial businesses in the area. Carl Hum, former director of The Mayor's Office of Industrial and Manufacturing Businesses told reporters, "The [Department of City Planning] certainly has its view about where the city and development were headed [...] I think in their view, they were fully convinced that manufacturing doesn't have a place in New York, and that better uses out there were for residential or commercial use" (Rosenberg 2014). Loss of industrial business compounds the pressure of rising housing costs, as these businesses provide essential, well-paying, accessible jobs for many of Williamsburg and Greenpoint's long-time residents, particularly Latinos and other minorities. Today, even the boutique manufacturing uses highlighted as successes of the IBZ, such as Brooklyn Brewery, struggle to remain in the area as land values and commercial rents continue to rise.[13]

The rezoning had a significant ripple affect on adjacent industrial areas. The Domino Sugar Factory, which had been home to hundreds of jobs for decades, was sold to a residential developer in 2004, while the city's rezoning was under review. The city responded to resident concerns that rezonings could spread to other industrial areas by maintaining that they had no intention of including the Domino property. City officials told *The New York Times* "that they were committed to finding an industrial reuse for the site." The director of the Brooklyn DCP office said the agency would consider future rezoning of industrial areas to the north, in the opposite direction of the Domino plant. Ten years later, the city approved a rezoning for the residential conversion and large-scale redevelopment of the site.

# OUT-OF-SCALE DEVELOPMENT AND THE 2008 CONTEXTUAL REZONING

While the 2005 waterfront rezoning allowed for new residential towers and upscale hotels, development was ramping up throughout the surrounding parts of Williamsburg. Under existing zoning and special permits, a number of "finger buildings" emerged—narrow buildings several stories taller than adjacent single-family homes and multi-family walk-up buildings. At the same time, housing advocates and community activists continued to push the city on the need for zoning and housing protections for existing affordable housing in low-income and communities of color in these neighborhoods.

The 2005 rezoning was the big shock that rattled the community, but it was followed by several smaller quakes. The first of these was the 2008 Greenpoint-Williamsburg Contextual Rezoning, which included 175 blocks in central Williamsburg and parts of Greenpoint, downzoned much of the previously mid-density residential area while allowing for some increased density along commercial corridors. Similar to the rezoning template followed in other communities, zoning protections were offered to lower density, higher-income blocks, while blocks with more multi-family housing and higher concentrations of low-income residents were upzoned or not rezoned at all. Despite the city's explicit argument that the rezoning would address out-of-context development and help protect existing affordable housing, the plan again excluded much of the lower-income and Latino part of South Williamsburg. The plan also relied on voluntary affordable housing incentives, not firm mandates.[14]

The 2005 rezoning continues to produce new luxury housing and displace existing industries and residents today. Most recently, the city approved the large-scale Greenpoint Landing project, which will include 10 luxury towers and thousands of units, thousands of square feet of commercial space, and a new park. Two smaller buildings will include approximately

**80**

## 03.I Greenpoint-Williamsburg Contextual Rezoning, 2009.

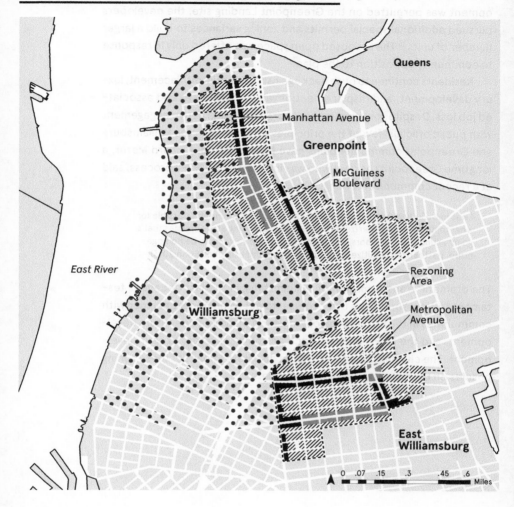

Queens

Manhattan Avenue

**Greenpoint**

McGuiness
Boulevard

East River

Rezoning
Area

**Williamsburg**

Metropolitan
Avenue

**East
Williamsburg**

0   .07   .15      .3      .45   .6
Miles

2005 Rezoning

Upzoned Residential

Upzoned Commercial

Downzoned Commercial

New York City Department of City Planning, December 2015.

200 units of income-targeted housing (Dai 2014). While high-rise development was permitted on the Greenpoint Landing site, the developers pursued additional special permits and zoning variances to build a larger number of units.[15] The proposed open space was offered only in response to community opposition to the plan.

Residents continue to push back against residential displacement, luxury development, and displacement of valued businesses and associated job loss. Despite robust community organizing and active engagement with public officials, few of the principles established in the Williamsburg and Greenpoint community plans have been realized. Richard Mazur, a longtime Greenpoint resident who was involved in the 197-a process, said at a recent community meeting:

> I was naive in 1995 to think that community-based planning was possible for what to do with our waterfront [...] What you're looking at is a species that's going extinct. My neighbors, my neighborhood, we're going to be homogenized, pasteurized, sanitized and supersized out of existence (Rinn 2013).

The dramatic transformation of Williamsburg in the last decade is testament to New York City's utter refusal to act as an honest partner with communities in the formulation of long-term plans to guide future development, and the DCP's blind reliance on zoning as a tool to spur development. The city has not addressed the disparate impact of these zoning policies on Latinos and low-income people.

## Endnotes

1. City Planning Commission, N 050110(A) ZRK, Report, March 14, 2005/Calendar No. 6, http://www.nyc.gov/html/dcp/pdf/cpc/050110a.pdf.

2. See Chapter Six for an explanation of 197-a plans.

3. City Planning Commission, N 050110(A) ZRK, Report, March 14, 2005/Calendar No. 6, accessed January 23, 2016.

4. City Planning Commission, N 050110(A) ZRK, Report, March 14, 2005/Calendar No. 6, accessed January 23, 2016, http://www.nyc.gov/html/dcp//pdf/cpc/050110a.pdf.

5. New York City Department of City Planning, "Chapter 27: Response to Public Comment," Greenpoint-Williamsburg Rezoning Environmental Impact Statement, accessed January 23, 2016, http://home.nyc.gov/html/dcp/pdf/greenpointwill/gw_feis_ch_27.pdf.

6. Philip DePaolo, "Hundreds to Demonstrate at Williamsburg-Greenpoint Waterfront for Affordable Housing," *Press Release*, November 18, 2004.

7. "Greenpoint-Williamsburg: Affordable Housing," accessed January 23, 2016, http://www.nyc.gov/html/dcp/html/greenpointwill/greenaffordhouse.shtml.

8. New York City Department of City Planning, "Chapter 27: Response to Public Comment," Greenpoint-Williamsburg Rezoning Environmental Impact Statement, accessed January 23, 2016, http://home.nyc.gov/html/dcp/pdf/greenpointwill/gw_feis_ch_27.pdf.

9. U.S. Census Bureau, Table PL-P2 CD: Total Population, Under 18 and 18 Years and Over by Mutually Exclusive Race and Hispanic Origin and Total Housing Units, New York City Community Districts, 1990 to 2010.

10. In addition, just 13 percent of all housing units built are permanently rent-regulated.

    Office of Council Member Antonio Reynoso, *Lessons from Williamsburg and Bushwick: Mandatory Inclusionary Zoning and Affordable Housing Development*, January 2016, accessed February 29, 2016, http://www.council.nyc.gov/d34/documents/Reynoso%20-%20Lessons%20from%20 Williamsburg%20and%20Bushwick.pdf.

11. Elizabeth Elizalde, "In Williamsburg, Efforts to Preserve Latino Culture," *Brooklyn News Service*, May 22, 2013, accessed February 29, 2016, http://journalism.blog.brooklyn.edu/in-williamsburg-efforts-to-preserve-latino-culture.

12. Elizabeth Elizalde, "In Williamsburg, Efforts to Preserve Latino Culture," *Brooklyn News Service*, May 22, 2013, accessed February 29, 2016, http://journalism.blog.brooklyn.edu/in-williamsburg-efforts-to-preserve-latino-culture.

13. Daniel Geiger, "Brooklyn Brewery Mulls Leaving Longtime Home in Williamsburgh for Elsewhere in the Borough," *Crain's New York Business*, February 23, 2016, accessed February 29, 2016, http://www.crainsnewyork.com/article/20160223/REAL_ESTATE/160229959/brooklyn-brewery-mulls-leaving-longtime-home-in-williamsburg-for.

    Alexandra Leon, "Brooklyn Brewery Says 'We're Not Leaving' Williamsburg Despite Rumors," *DNAInfo*, February 25, 2016, accessed February 29, 2016, https://www.dnainfo.com/new-york/20160225/williamsburg/brooklyn-brewery-says-were-not-leaving-williamsburg-despite-rumors.

14. City Planning Commission, C 090334 ZMK, Report, July 1, 2009/Calendar No. 13, accessed January 23, 2016, http://www.nyc.gov/html/dcp/pdf/cpc/090334.pdf.

15. City Planning Commission, N 140028 ZRK, Report, November 6, 2013/Calendar No. 6, accessed January 23, 2016, http://www.nyc.gov/html/dcp/pdf/cpc/140028.pdf.

# CHAPTER FOUR

# HARLEM: DISPLACEMENT, NOT INTEGRATION

## SYLVIA MORSE

**04.A Swing Low, a memorial to Harriet Tubman, by Alison Saar.**

*Installed in 2008 on Frederick Douglass Boulevard. Photo: Sylvia Morse, 2016*

Since 2003, city-backed rezonings have ushered in thousands of new, mostly higher-income and white residents to the historically affordable, black neighborhood of Harlem. On the surface, this might appear to be a positive step towards racial integration. However, the widely held notion that statistically mixed neighborhoods by themselves will end racial discrimination, segregation, and inequality is largely unsupported (Cheshire 2007). The 2003 Frederick Douglass Boulevard and 2009 125th Street Corridor rezonings, in particular, have raised land values and increased real estate speculation, resulting in the displacement of longtime black and Latino residents and businesses. Instead of helping to "integrate" Harlem, the rezonings are expanding the white community on the west side of Manhattan at the expense of the people of color who have lived in and built the community.

The rezonings continue the city's history, dating back to the 19th century, of pushing black residents out of lower Manhattan and, later, Midtown. Now they are being pushed out of Harlem.

**86**

The Frederick Douglass Boulevard rezoning spurred the development of residential towers and renovation of low-rise housing for luxury markets. The City Planning Commission's approval of the Frederick Douglass rezoning did not mention race. The rezoning proposal did not address Harlem's role as a historically and predominantly black neighborhood, nor present the rezoning as a tool for achieving racial integration, nor forecast racial impacts at all. Simply put, the city did not plan for the racially disparate impacts of the rezoning in Harlem. In the 125th Street Rezoning, facing mounting local opposition, city planners did respond to resident concerns of displacement, but even these responses remained race neutral.

The gentrification of Harlem was driven largely by economic factors that ignored and threatened the neighborhood's significance as an African American cultural and economic mecca. However, zoning and housing policies played a powerful role by increasing displacement pressures in this community that had thrived despite decades of city neglect. As a result, Harlem's black population is at its lowest in a century and is continuing to decline, while many remaining black and Latino residents face rising rents, landlord harassment, racist and violent policing, and stagnant incomes. Small black-owned businesses that provide affordable services, hubs for community engagement, and local jobs are also being displaced by residential development and skyrocketing commercial rents. New Harlem residents, most of them white and upper-income, are afforded the benefits

**04.B Neighborhood Map:**
**Central Harlem—Manhattan**
**Community Board 10**

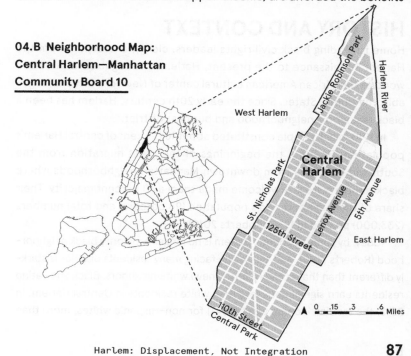

**04.C Typical low-rise housing in Harlem.**

*Photo: Sylvia Morse, 2016*

of better amenities and safer streets, living in enclaves largely immune to the challenges facing their neighbors.

The multiple rezoning actions did not reduce segregation but only strengthened its hold.

# HISTORY AND CONTEXT

Home to leading black civil rights leaders, clergy, and artists from the Harlem Renaissance to the present, Harlem is recognized around the world as the African American cultural center of New York City and, argu-ably, the United States. Since the early 20th century, Harlem has been a black residential neighborhood and business district.

In 1910, black people constituted about 10 percent of central Harlem's population. By 1930, the beginnings of the great migration from the South and the influx from downtown Manhattan neighborhoods where black people were less welcome made them a 70 percent majority. Their share of the neighborhood's population (98 percent) and total numbers (233,000) peaked in 1950 (Roberts 2010).

Today, by some accounts, Harlem is no longer a majority black neighbor-hood (Roberts 2010). And the reality facing many residents of color is stark-ly different than that of their (mostly new) white neighbors. Black and Latino residents earn significantly less than white residents in Central Harlem: in 2013, the median income was $82,411 for non-Hispanic whites, more than

**88**

**04.D New residential development in the Frederick Douglass Boulevard upzoned area.**

*Photo: Sylvia Morse, 2016*

twice the median income of black residents ($33,289) and Latinos ($27,804).[1] The area continues to face high rates of poverty amidst the rising cost of living (Furman Center 2014).

Harlem has a widely varied housing stock ranging from low-rise walk-ups to mid-size apartment complexes. There are Mitchell-Lama rental and cooperative buildings and a large stock of public housing. Now, glass condominium and rental towers and large shopping complexes are beginning to shape the Harlem landscape as well, particularly in the Frederick Douglass and 125th Street rezoning areas, where real estate values have skyrocketed in recent decades.

Public planning policies have long threatened the quality of life, residential stability, and community health and cohesion of black Harlemites. In the mid-20th century, urban renewal plans displaced many poor black residents from so-called slum housing in order to create new large-scale housing and commercial development. Redevelopment, however, did not usually benefit those it displaced. Many who lost their homes were not able to relocate locally. Those who were able to secure residence in new public housing were often subject to discrimination and racial steering. Harlem's public housing developments were majority black and Latino, while white residents secured housing in other neighborhoods with more economic and political resources (Dagen Bloom 2009).

The city's massive investments in parks and other infrastructure under Robert Moses largely excluded Harlem, with less than a quarter of investments made above 100th Street. Later, during the city's fiscal crisis of the

1970s, disinvestment led thousands of landlords to abandon their properties; the city became the owner by default and did a poor job improving conditions. For decades, absent sufficient city investment and facing high rates of poverty, black Harlem residents built up their community with locally owned businesses and community organizations (Gill 2011).

This successful community-led investment helped lay the groundwork for private real estate-led development in the 1990s and early 2000s, which once again put Harlem's black residents at risk. In the 1970s, the city owned two-thirds of Harlem's developable property; many properties were sold at auction to speculative developers, sometimes as large, consolidated parcels (Gill 2011, 411). The city's goal was to sell off publicly owned land in order to spur development (Gorrild et al. 2008). While these parcels could have been used to subsidize much-needed low-income housing, the city instead cut back on collaborations with community-based non-profit groups. As city (and federal) policy shifted the focus of affordable housing development to middle-income housing, those non-profits that could secure partnerships with the city followed suit (Little 2002). Also during this period, the federal and state governments cut capital and operating funds for public housing. Thus, market-rate housing development took off while the low- and moderate-income housing stock aged and dwindled. In the late 1990s, local elected officials and business leaders helped launch a federally backed economic development program known as the Upper Manhattan Empowerment Zone (UMEZ), which brought large-scale commercial redevelopment and multinational retail corporations to Harlem's

**04.E  HarlemUSA commercial development.**

*In 1998, the Upper Manhattan Empowerment Zone brought some of the first multinational chain stores to 125th Street. Photo: Sylvia Morse, 2016*

historic 125th Street (Hyra 2008). The commercial corridor, once known for black-owned specialty shops and street vendors, began to look like "some alter ego of a middle-American mall" (Hyra 2008; Little 2002).

By the early 2000s, the pressures of gentrification had intensified and there was a growing awareness of the plans being advanced by the city and developers. In the summer of 2002, residents organized rallies and town halls and formed a community-led housing task force to push public officials to address rising housing costs. Despite vocal public engagement on the issue of displacement, the city remained focused on enhancing real estate opportunities and subsidizing upper-middle and high-income housing. The city then embarked on the first large-scale rezoning of Harlem since the 1961 Zoning Resolution—the Frederick Douglass Boulevard Rezoning.

## THE FREDERICK DOUGLASS BOULEVARD REZONING

In 2003, the Department of City Planning (DCP) proposed to rezone 44 blocks of Central Harlem to promote residential and commercial growth. Citing Harlem's growing population and new development, much of which was out of scale with the surrounding townhouses and small apartment buildings, DCP's stated goals were to "address Harlem's growing need for new housing" and expand commercial uses for this "growing community."[2] DCP's approach included residential upzonings on the avenues and main streets, while introducing contextual zones on the mid-blocks to promote conformity with the existing low-rise housing. The rezoning aimed to increase ground-floor retail with new commercial overlays on the high-traffic 116th Street.[3] Ultimately, the plan increased the residential capacity of the rezoning area's 44 blocks by 50 percent, or 6,713,744 square feet.

The rezoning supported real estate market trends, benefitting property owners and speculative investors without including protections for tenants.

## 04.F Frederick Douglas Boulevard Rezoning, 2003.

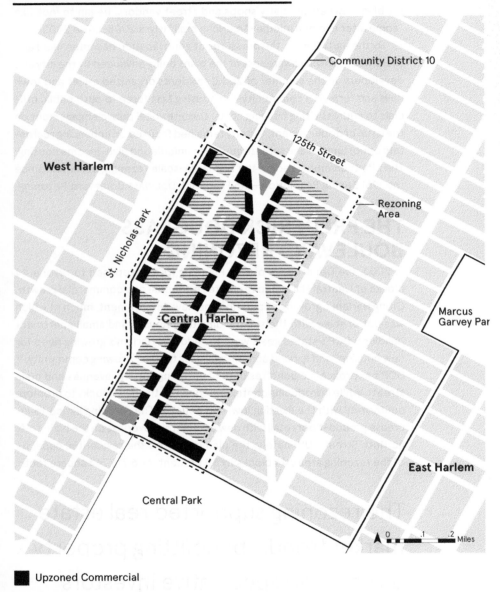

Community District 10

125th Street

West Harlem

St. Nicholas Park

Rezoning Area

Central Harlem

Marcus Garvey Par

East Harlem

Central Park

0   .1   .2 Miles

■ Upzoned Commercial

■ Upzoned Residential

≣ Downzoned Residential (Contexual)

New York City Department of City Planning, December 2015.

This growth, however, would not affect all parts of the community uniformly. The population growth analysis and related rezoning proposal presented by DCP did not include income or racial data to address demographic shifts and types of housing needs. The rezoning supported real estate market trends, benefitting property owners and speculative investors without including protections for tenants.

In the context of the city's hot residential market, owners of low-density housing and commercial buildings in upzoned areas would have incentives to sell their properties as development sites for new residential buildings. Luxury development on these sites and on vacant lots would also increase land values and rents in surrounding blocks. The contextual downzoning to "preserve [side street] blockfronts"[4] would limit denser residential development in those areas, but it put tenants at risk by protecting the rising property values of townhouses (Rich 2003). Harlem had low rates of black homeownership, and many residents rented small units or single rooms in structures built as one- and two-family homes (Feltz 2008). Absent significant affordable housing preservation programs, both the upzoning and downzoning components of this plan threatened low- and moderate-income renters.

## RESIDENTS RAISE THE ISSUE OF DISPLACEMENT

In the months leading up to the Frederick Douglass Boulevard rezoning, residents expressed their concerns about rising housing costs and limited availability. Sharon Wilson, a long-time Harlem resident and city employee, for instance, told reporters in 2002 that, "remaining in the community seems impossible [...] Generally, one-bedroom rentals that once would have been considered high at $500 now go for $1,300 to $1,500 [per month]." In the year before the rezoning, unlawful evictions and pressure on rent-stabilized tenants were on the rise. As resident organizer Nellie Bailey told *The Village Voice*, "We have seen a sharp increase in people losing their apartments due to landlord harassment for problems other than non-payment [...] Money is in the air and everybody wants to get on the gentrification bandwagon" (Little 2002).

Affordable housing development was not a strong component of the plan. The DCP objectives for the rezoning included "foster[ing] new opportunities for residential development" accessible across income ranges, but did not name income-targeted housing as an outcome in many public documents related to the rezoning.[5] The plan did include height and bulk bonuses for projects that utilized the optional Quality Housing program to set aside income-targeted housing units, but voluntary affordable housing programs have historically created few affordable units, especially absent additional subsidy (Madar 2015; Dulchin, Gates and Williams 2014).

The city did not include a robust affordable housing program even though residents were clearly demanding it in the public review process that preceded the rezoning. Residents expressed concerns about the lack of low-income housing programs in public meetings with multiple city agencies, some of them unrelated to the rezoning. The city's position, as one reporter put it, was that "it's not worth sinking low-income subsidies into a community where housing can easily sell at market rate" with the right zoning incentives (Little 2002). A representative of the Department of Housing Preservation and Development (HPD) told the reporter, "In a world of finite resources, government is intended to spur a private market where it is not working on its own." HPD is not responsible for zoning, but does shape city housing policies and programs that play a central role in supporting public and private housing investment. In Harlem, HPD contended that there was a more-than-adequate supply of low-income housing that was not threatened by emerging real estate interests (Little 2002).

The city's position, as one reporter put it, was that 'It's not worth sinking low-income subsidies into a community where housing can easily sell at market rate' with the right zoning incentives.

Despite growing concern at the time of the rezoning around gentrification and the need for affordable housing, the plan drew little political opposition. Residents did not organize against the plan in great numbers, and as a result, political representatives did not push back on the plan. The community board unanimously supported the rezoning. The CPC unanimously approved the plan at a public hearing absent public comment.[6]

**94**

Given the widespread concerns with affordable housing and displacement that were expressed at other forums at the time of the rezoning, why did the plan receive such a muted public response? Many residents may not have been aware of the plan: the DCP under Bloomberg primarily disseminated zoning information through community boards, which have limited reach and disproportionate engagement from older residents and homeowners. This rezoning was among the earliest of the Bloomberg administration's nearly 140 rezonings and many may not have been familiar with the complex land use review process or the plan's potential impacts. Another reason could be the solid support for the rezoning by the Harlem political establishment.

## THE IMPACT OF THE REZONING: NEW UPSCALE DEVELOPMENT AND LESS AFFORDABLE HOUSING

The Frederick Douglass rezoning substantially increased the residential and commercial development capacity in a low-income black neighborhood already struggling with rising housing costs and displacement. Simultaneously, the rezoning failed to include strong provisions for the creation and preservation of low- and middle-income housing. The rezoning resulted in the displacement of residents and also began to reshape the commercial landscape, community networks, and cultural life of geographic Harlem.

After the rezoning, "development took off," according to a report by *The Real Deal* magazine. New upscale housing, hotel, and commercial construction was initially concentrated along the newly upzoned Frederick Douglass Boulevard, with every investment inviting another. A representative of the Harlem office of the Corcoran real estate group said, "We think it's an absolutely great location, primarily because we are in a development corridor" (Strozier 2015).

By 2009, there were "probably 15 or 20 new condo or co-op buildings that [had] popped up between 110th and 125th along Frederick Douglass Boulevard in the past six or seven years," according to a Harlem-based realtor (Arieff 2009). By 2012, according to an account in *The New York Times*, "when condos hit the market, they go quickly, with the average price for a one-bedroom at about a half-million dollars" (Gregory 2012).

These new developments were outside of the price range of the average Harlem resident, and the new units were not marketed to them.

**04.G Various housing developments along the upzoned Frederick Douglass Boulevard.**

Photos: Sylvia Morse, 2016

The Livmor, for instance, a luxury condominium on Frederick Douglass Boulevard built after the rezoning, offered:

> one-, two- and three-bedroom apartments from 808 to 2,100 square feet and priced from the mid $400,000s to $1.1 million or $1.2 million, some with private roof terraces. Amenities [...] include a yoga studio, a media room with projection TV, a children's play space and a kitchen for catered events (Arieff 2009).

A real estate executive managing the sales explains their marketing approach and target demographic, and confirms that the rezoned area is essentially an extension of the Upper West Side:

> I consider the Franklin (sic) Douglass Boulevard corridor to be an extension of the Upper West Side at this point [...] Many years ago, some people said you couldn't go above 68th Street, and now it is even above 125th Street. [Buyers at the Livmor are] people who are perhaps priced out of the Upper West Side. It is like any emerging neighborhood [...] People have been moving to these various areas because of the attraction of the size of the apartments and the affordability of the product"(Arieff 2009).

Another Harlem realtor echoed this viewpoint, saying, "Any buyer that comes up here is going to spend much less than in other parts of the city and get more, and these luxury buildings are attracting *a wider audience*" (emphasis added) (Arieff 2009). In other words, new residential development explicitly targeted higher income households moving into the neighborhood, rather than creating new rental or homeownership opportunities for Harlem's longtime, mostly black residents even as they called for the preservation and development of low- and moderate-income housing.

# New residential development explicitly targeted higher income households moving into the neighborhood, rather than creating new rental or homeownership opportunities for Harlem's longtime, mostly black residents.

Existing low-rise apartment buildings, many of them rent-stabilized, and townhouses were redeveloped for the new upscale market as well, particularly in the contextual downzoning area. A growing luxury market for historic townhouses, bolstered by zoning that preserves the low density neighborhood character, would lead to the conversion of much of this housing to single-family owner-occupied housing for higher-income households (Maurasse 2006, 102).

Almost 10 years after the rezoning, more than 1,100 housing units were created in the rezoning area, mostly along Frederick Douglass Boulevard. A small fraction of these are affordable or income-targeted (Slatin 2012). Within the rezoning area, median monthly gross rent increased by 58 percent, as compared to a 16 percent increase for all of Manhattan (Goldberg 2015).

## RESIDENTIAL DISPLACEMENT AND DISPARATE RACIAL IMPACTS

When the rezoning took place in 2003, Harlem was already experiencing gentrification pressures, which weighed most heavily on the neighborhood's black and Latino residents. Since then, housing costs and displacement pressures have escalated dramatically. By 2004, Central Harlem had among the city's highest rates of residential displacement and homeless shelter entry. Townhouses that were once subdivided to create multiple rental units were increasingly sold for occupancy as single-family homes.[7] A 2006 survey found that 58.2 percent of Harlem residents knew someone who was forced to move from their home because of rising rents (Maurasse 2006, 81, 102). And, while the city currently has no mechanism to track displacement due to rent increases or landlord harassment, US Census data gives a sense of the demographic shifts in neighborhood. From 2000 to 2013, in the Frederick Douglass Boulevard rezoning area, the total population increased by 18 percent; the white population increased 455 percent while the black population declined by 5 percent, and the Latino population declined by 13 percent (Goldberg 2015).

Many residents expressed the concern that low- and middle-income African Americans were being pushed out. One Harlem tenant organizer told *The Washington Post*: "Things have gotten a little out of hand, yes, they have […] So many people endured the bad times and can't afford the good."[8]

From 2000 to 2013, in the Frederick Douglass Boulevard rezoning area, the total population increased by 18 percent; the white population increased 455 percent while the black population declined by 5 percent, and the Latino population declined by 13 percent.

According to long-time Harlem business owner Melba Wilson:

> Change isn't always bad, but I don't want it to become a place where the original people are no longer welcome here, that they can no longer afford to be in a place that they built (Gregory 2012).

The displacement of black residents is evident in daily life on the streets of the neighborhood and in the numbers. According to American Community Survey and census data, from 2000 to 2010, "Central Harlem's population [grew] more than in any other decade since the 1940s, [...] but its black population [...] is smaller than at any time since the 1920s" (Roberts 2010). In 2008, about one-fifth of Harlem's white residents had entered their Harlem residence within the last year, whereas just 7 percent of black households had recently moved in (Roberts 2010). Bernard Moore, a black Harlem resident, succinctly captured the multiple ways new development shut out many moderate income and black residents. First, he told a *Reuters* reporter, new construction produced few local jobs because projects use outside and non-union crews. Second, residential development drives up rents and land values. "The cost of rent is so high," he said, "even churches are selling their buildings to prospective apartment buildings that are out of reach for most black folks" (Trotta 2006).

**04.H The famed Melba's restaurant and new housing on Frederick Douglass Boulevard.**

*Photo: Sylvia Morse, 2016*

## 04.I  Falling Black Population, Growing White Population in the Frederick Douglas Boulevard Rezoning Area, 2000–2013.

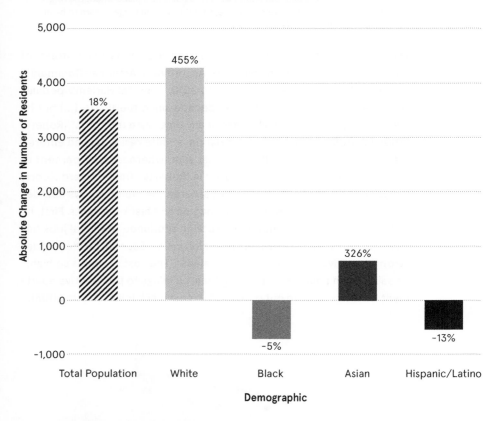

*Percentages represent the percent change in number of residents within a demographic between 2000 and 2013.

Leo Goldberg, based on U.S. Census Bureau, American Community Survey 2013 data.

# MORE REZONINGS AND REDEVELOPMENT PLANS, AND COMMUNITY RESISTANCE

The 2003 Frederick Douglass Boulevard rezoning spurred new development in Central Harlem. DCP ushered in additional rezonings to further expand development. There was no hint that DCP took into account the disparate racial impacts of the 2003 rezoning in formulating subsequent actions.

In addition to the Frederick Douglass Boulevard, 125th Street, and Special Manhattanville District rezonings discussed here, rezoning actions in East Harlem and West Harlem also introduced new development to the area.

In 2006, Columbia University announced plans to develop 17 acres of educational, residential, commercial, and hotel uses in West Harlem, neighboring the Frederick Douglass Boulevard rezoning area (Williams 2006). The plan would displace hundreds of residents and businesses through the use of eminent domain and other property deals. Residents and advocates resisted the expansion of this wealthy private institution, which had a checkered history of community engagement and collaboration. Community organizers again emphasized the ongoing problem of residential displacement and the need for low-income affordable housing. In 2007, following deals that aimed to expand income-targeted housing provisions and community access, the city approved the Special Manhattanville District for the Columbia University Expansion Plan (Moynihan 2007). At the same time, the CPC approved a 197-a plan for Manhattanville, which the city recognizes only as advisory and has no duty to implement despite formal adoption. The 197-a plan did, however, provide a cover of community support for the city-backed plan, just as in Greenpoint and Williamsburg (see Chapter Three).

Columbia's expansion, in tandem with the 2003 rezoning and zoning and housing policy that incentivized real estate development, coincided with the continued harassment and displacement of tenants (Moss 2015). For instance, tenants at 3333 Broadway, a large affordable housing complex that saw an influx of Columbia students and other new residents paying market rents, sued management for withholding services from tenants with rental subsidies (Del Signore 2008; Morgenson 2008). Resident and housing voucher recipient Ray Anthony, whose rent went up from $470 per month in 1998 to $3,700 in 2009, told the press that he had seen:

> 100 black and Latino families [move] out since the new management took over. "We are the low-income people," he said, "white people got no problem paying the rent." (Keshner 2009).

## 04.J Harlem Area Rezonings under the Bloomberg Administration.

*In addition to the Frederick Douglass Boulevard, 125th Street, and Special Manhattanville District rezonings discussed here, rezoning actions in East Harlem and West Harlem also introduced new development to the area.*

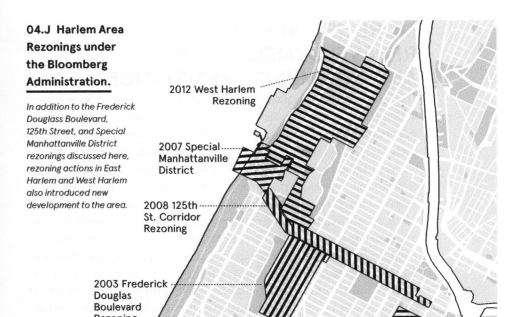

2012 West Harlem Rezoning

2007 Special Manhattanville District

2008 125th St. Corridor Rezoning

2003 Frederick Douglas Boulevard Rezoning

2003 East Harlem Rezoning

0 .1 .2 .4 .6 miles

New York City Department of City Planning, NYC GIS Zoning Features, December 2015.

Next came another large-scale rezoning plan that rocked the neighborhood: the 125th Street Corridor rezoning. In 2007, DCP proposed to rezone the historic commercial and cultural center of Harlem and adjacent streets "from river to river" for high-rise residential and new commercial use. The community was organized, well versed in zoning policy, and facing ever more dire challenges to maintaining housing and community. Resident activists brought hundreds of residents to public meetings and published responses to claims from public officials on the rezoning proposal. Activist Nellie Bailey, for instance, wrote a clarification of the city's affordable housing claims, explaining that:

> approximately 3,858 luxury units are projected for development in the 24 blocks footprint that expands from 2nd Avenue to Broadway between 124th and 127th Streets. Despite [local City Council Member Inez] Dickens' false assertion that 46% of these units are being "income-targeted" only 5%, or 200 units are for families earning below $30,000" (Bailey 2008).

This plan, like the Frederick Douglass Boulevard rezoning, only included voluntary incentives for affordable housing, which developers could choose not to employ. The plan was designed to capitalize on and maximize real estate interest, which was already squeezing out black and Latino residents. The announcement of the rezoning alone increased that speculation. As local State Assemblyman Keith Wright, a proponent of the plan, said:

> Folks want to build higher right now [...] You have some rather large vacant lots that are being held onto by private developers, and they're just waiting for the proposed rezoning (Brown 2007).

Residents again warned public officials that the upzoning would cause the direct and indirect displacement of small black-owned businesses, including 125th Street's famed street vendors, as well as residents. Many residents and community groups made it known that they wanted to be involved in the planning of their community, but the city did not offer seats at the decision-making table. Despite City Planning's claim that the plan reflected more than four years of community meetings, many residents and business owners stated that they had no meaningful input in the plan. Instead, they saw the city's planning process as mere "social engineering" (Williams 2008). Many of the most active critics of the plan stated that the city's representation of its community engagement efforts was overblown. This was the experience of historian and Harlem activist Michael Henry Adams:

The city ignored his suggestion to include preservation in the rezoning plan and to landmark historic buildings that were important in the Harlem Renaissance and civil rights struggles. After it invited him to a planning meeting once, Adams said he never heard from the city again. He did notice that his name is listed on the Department of City Planning's website as one of the "stakeholders, property owners, residents and elected officials" who held more than 150 meetings to discuss and refine the plan (Feltz 2008).

Activists also challenged the claims of community support for the plan that came primarily from representatives of business and cultural institutions that would receive funding or bonuses related to the plan. The city needed the backing of institutions that support African American history and art, but did not address or attempt to mitigate the displacement, financial burden, and stress that residents experienced as a result of residential and business loss and its impact on black cultural institutions. As Michael Henry Adams put it, "If the only black presence in Harlem is a memory in the form of museums and place names, to hell with that" (Feltz 2008).

Feeling their recommendations were being ignored by the city, Harlem activists protested and held community meetings that brought out thousands, made public comments at meetings, and launched lawsuits (Amzallag 2008).

**04.K The trendy Aloft Hotel opened on Frederick Douglass Boulevard and 123rd Street in 2011, following the 125th Street Corridor rezoning.**

*Photo: Sylvia Morse, 2016*

**04.L** In a protest against the 125th Street rezoning organized by Coalition to Save Harlem on April 12, 2008, residents formed a human chain from "river to river," along the proposed rezoning area.

**04.M** Vera Wilson, the owner of House of Seafood restaurant, faced eviction due to speculation around the rezoning of 125th St.

*Photos: Rezoning Harlem. Film. Directed by Natasha Florentino and Tamara Gubernat. New York: Third World News Reel, 2008.*

**04.N Typical existing retail on 125th Street.**

*Photo: Sylvia Morse, 2016*

Outside of formal organizing, the topic took over the daily and emotional lives of many residents. In 2008 at the time of the rezoning, *The New York Times* reported that:

> apprehension about gentrification has become a constant, and is now a common theme at Sunday church services and a standard topic of conversation in barber shops and beauty salons, on street corners, in bars, at public housing community rooms and among the doormen of the neighborhood's new condominium buildings (Williams 2008).

Human service organizations reported a growing number of incidences of "insomnia and hypertension related to fears about losing [ones] home" (Williams 2008).

Small businesses that provide affordable services and often serve as cultural landmarks are also being evicted by new development facilitated by the rezoning. Harlem has been a thriving center of long-time black-owned and African immigrant businesses, including street vendors, that serve community interests and price-points, while providing local employment. Since the rezonings, many local businesses were directly displaced by new development or driven out by rising rents.

**106**

"This gentrification is affecting us mentally," said Kaaw Sow, a representative of a Senegalese business association, describing the impact of rising costs on the local economy and community to a reporter. As *New African* magazine reported, "[Sow] says the arrival of wealthy whites has pushed rents in the area up and led the landlord who owns the Association's storefront offices to raise the rent from $1,300 per month to close to $6,000 dollars." (Goffe 2014).

In place of these businesses there are now multi-national chain stores and high-end boutiques. *The New York Times* described the transformation in 2012: "Now, along today's [Frederick Douglass] boulevard sit an organic products store, a sushi restaurant and a yoga studio with toddler and tween classes" (Gregory 2012). *New African* magazine highlighted the racial impact of this change, including the cultural tourism and nostalgia that characterizes some of the new businesses:

> It's clear Harlem is no longer a local black people's haven. It is, instead, a hotspot for high income hipsters attracted by the neighbourhood's high quality architecture and by the easy commute to New York City's commercial and business districts downtown. Harlem is a hotspot, too, for interlopers eager to experience the urban, uptown African-American experience close up and in person"(Goffe 2014).

Today, Harlem residents and advocates continue to fight to preserve affordable housing and black-owned businesses. However, the impact of the city's rezonings is clear: the population of Central Harlem, the area most affected by rezonings, grew 9 percent in a decade, while its black population fell 12 percent and white population ballooned by more than 400 percent. The disparate racial impacts of development spurred by the rezoning are shown clearly in the numbers, but also in the words of longtime black residents who have watched their family, friends, and neighbors pushed out of the black community they built in the midst of discrimination and service cutbacks by the city, all the while fearing for the loss of their own homes. As Michael Henry Adams said, "I'm not suggesting that Harlem will cease to exist once people are gone [...] it will be a different place. It will be a diminished place that is not as rich a contributor to American culture and history and heritage" (Feltz 2008).

**Endnotes**

1. In 2013, the median household income in Central Harlem was $36,889 compared to the citywide median of $52,259.

2. US Census Bureau, American Community Survey, 2009–2013 Estimates, SE:T58. Median Household Income By Race (in 2013 Inflation Adjusted Dollars).

3. "Frederick Douglass Boulevard Rezoning Proposal - Approved!: REZONING OBJECTIVES," Department of City Planning, accessed January 18, 2016, http://www.nyc.gov/html/dcp/html/fdb/fdb1.shtml.

4. City Planning Commission, "C 030436 ZMM," September 10, 2003/Calendar No. 19, accessed January 11, 2016, http://www.nyc.gov/html/dcp/pdf/cpc/030436.pdf.

5. "Frederick Douglass Boulevard Rezoning Proposal - Approved!: REZONING OBJECTIVES," Department of City Planning, accessed January 18, 2016, http://www.nyc.gov/html/dcp/html/fdb/fdb1.shtml.

5. "Frederick Douglass Boulevard Rezoning Proposal - Approved!: REZONING OBJECTIVES," Department of City Planning, accessed January 18, 2016, http://www.nyc.gov/html/dcp/html/fdb/fdb1.shtml.

6. City Planning Commission, "C 030436 ZMM," September 10, 2003/Calendar No. 19, accessed January 11, 2016, http://www.nyc.gov/html/dcp/pdf/cpc/030436.pdf.

7. Michael Powell, "Harlem's New Rush: Booming Real Estate," *The Washington Post*, March 13, 2005, accessed February 29, 2016, http://www.washingtonpost.com/wp-dyn/articles/A30280-2005Mar12.html.

8. Michael Powell, "Harlem's New Rush: Booming Real Estate," *The Washington Post*, March 13, 2005, accessed February 29, 2016, http://www.washingtonpost.com/wp-dyn/articles/A30280-2005Mar12.html.

# CHAPTER FIVE

# CHINATOWN: UNPROTECTED AND UNDONE

## SAMUEL STEIN[1]

For years, the immigrant and working-class neighborhood of Chinatown was able to resist gentrification, even as all nearby downtown neighborhoods turned into segregated citadels for the rich and the white. Today, in large part due to zoning actions taken by the city in 2008 and 2011, Chinatown is in the midst of a swift and severe transformation into yet another exclusive enclave.

First, a contextual "downzoning" that limited development in the neighboring affluent East Village, absent zoning protections for Chinatown, pushed development pressures further into Chinatown. The subsequent rezoning of a large parcel of public land for large-scale, high-end development was a missed opportunity to create low-income housing to help mitigate displacement, and instead created opportunities for new luxury units that bolster speculation in surrounding areas. Luxury development, rent deregulation, condo conversion, and tenement demolition have all increased significantly since these rezonings, resulting in declining Asian and Latino populations.

Attempts to create a community plan that would push back against these trends have so far been rebuffed by the de Blasio administration, which is moving forward with similar rezoning actions, despite evidence of their racially discriminatory impact. The city's refusal to take corrective action amounts to intentional discrimination against current residents and those who would be expected to reside in Chinatown if corrective fair housing measures were undertaken by the city.

# HISTORY AND CONTEXT

Chinatown and the Lower East Side have long been home to new immigrants and working-class communities. Chinatown is an economic and cultural hub for Chinese and other Asian communities that, over the past century and a half, has developed a complex and evolving network of migration, finance, employment, and land ownership, which, though far from ideal, has provided housing and jobs for generations of immigrants (Kwong 1996).

A recent report found that the neighborhood has 116,722 residents living in 2,118 buildings (AALDEF, 2013). According to 2013 American Community Survey data—figures that likely undercount immigrants—the racial composition of Community District 3 is 45 percent Asian, 19 percent white, 26 percent Hispanic, and 7 percent black. While the median income for the metro area is $64,786, the median income in Chinatown and the Lower East Side is just $37,996, and on several Chinatown blocks average income is closer to $16,000.

The average structure is a five-story tenement with stores on the ground floor. Most of these buildings were built in the 19th and early 20th centuries during one of the Lower East Side's immigration-driven population booms. Its far eastern edge is home to some of the city's first public housing projects, including Smith, LaGuardia, and Baruch Houses, as well as Confucius Plaza, a 762-unit Mitchell-Lama cooperative complex.

For nearly a century, New York City government and real estate interests have viewed Chinatown and the Lower East Side as opportunities for growth and development. Located in the heart of lower Manhattan, south of Midtown, and near the towers of Wall Street and the iconic East River bridges, these neighborhoods have been subject to one scheme after another aimed at spurring high-end construction and dispersing its population of working-class people of color (Lin 1998).

One of the first such schemes was the Lower Manhattan Expressway, a 1929 plan for an elevated highway that would have carried 120,000 cars per day from the Holland Tunnel to the Manhattan and Williamsburg bridges. Cutting through Canal, Broome, and Delancey streets, it would have displaced at least 2,000 families and 800 businesses employing 10,000 people. Over the years, the plan was supported by powerful city interests, including Robert Moses, the influential Regional Plan Association, Governor Rockefeller, and a group of finance and real estate interests known as the Lower Manhattan Association. Opposition, however, was furious and

**05.A Neighborhood Map: Chinatown—Manhattan Community District 3**

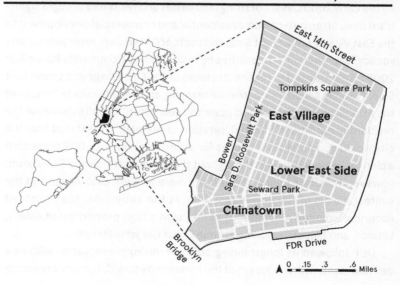

sustained, bringing together Chinatown community leaders with famed activist Jane Jacobs and her Greenwich Village allies (Flint 2009). The plan was eventually shelved, but the impulse to "redevelop" Chinatown lived on.

Many of the same public officials and business groups later came up with a Title 1 Urban Renewal proposal called "China Village." Declaring the neighborhood "one of the worst slums in New York," the State Housing Division proposed demolishing fifteen acres of Chinatown and replacing it with eight high-rise housing projects and an Orientalist tourist market (as quoted in Umbach and Wishnoff 2008, 220). In the face of opposition from Chinatown residents and dwindling finances, the plan was vastly scaled down, and resulted in a much smaller urban renewal action.

In 1981, the Department of City Planning (DCP) proposed a Special Manhattan Bridge District for Chinatown's east side. The plan would have encouraged the construction of private high-rise condominiums at prices very few Chinatown residents could afford. Several community organizations resisted the plan and sued the city; the most significant lawsuit, *Chinese Staff and Workers Association v. City of New York*, argued that environmental impact reviews must evaluate the secondary economic impacts of private development, including indirect displacement.[2] The judge sided with the community, and the rezoning plan was halted.

# 2008 REZONING AND DISPARATE RACIAL IMPACTS

By the early 2000s, years of rising land values and rents had brought significant new, often out-of-scale residential and commercial development to the East Village, Lower East Side, and parts of Chinatown. After years of advocacy for preservation measures by residents and Community Board 3, in 2008 DCP proposed to rezone 111 blocks of the East Village and Lower East Side. The plan called for contextual rezoning and height limits to "preserve the established neighborhood scale and character" as well as increase the residential density. In the final iteration of the plan, DCP stated that the city would also provide incentives for affordable housing.[3] DCP presented a plan for balanced growth throughout the Lower East Side and Chinatown; however, the downzoning covered the more affluent East Village and the whitest blocks of the Lower East Side. At the same time, the proposed upzoning included a number of blocks with a high proportion of Asians, Latinos, and blacks, including Avenue D and Chrystie Street.

DCP followed its longstanding policy of mixing preservation with new development, with the assent of the community board. The city's rezoning

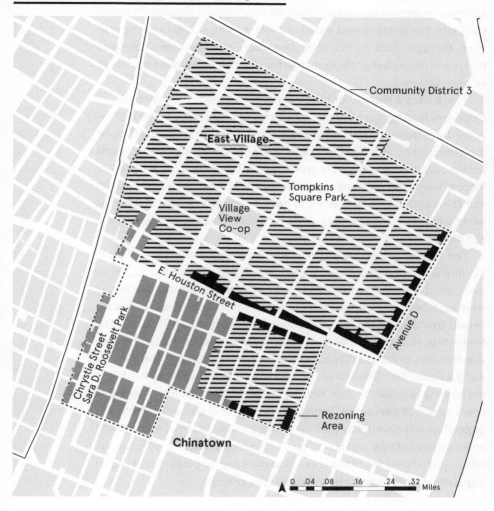

Community District 3

East Village

Tompkins
Square Park

Village
View
Co-op

E. Houston Street

Chrystie Street
Sara D. Roosevelt Park

Avenue D

Rezoning
Area

Chinatown

0   .04  .08      .16       .24     .32
Miles

▤ Downzoned Residential (Contextual)

■ Upzoned Commercial

■ Upzoned Residential

New York City Department of City Planning, NYC GIS Zoning Features, December 2015.

was sold to the community as a way to preserve the East Village's low-to-mid-rise residential character, and drive development towards its widest corridors. The upzoned area included a voluntary inclusionary zoning program, through which participating developers could receive a floor area bonus and/or tax benefit in exchange for allotting 20 percent of units as income-targeted.

There were a number of problems with this plan. The proposed inclusionary housing, for example, would create only a small number of income-targeted rental and condo apartments, and even those would be far too expensive for most neighborhood residents. Qualifying income ranges for the proposed housing were typically $43,000 to $61,500; the median income within the rezoning's boundaries was just over $25,600 (Angotti and Ervin 2008). This was bound to have a disparate racial outcome, as white incomes in the district greatly exceeded those of Asians, Latinos, and blacks.

The biggest problem with the plan, however, was what it excluded. Despite shared concerns over unmitigated development and displacement, most of Chinatown and the Lower East Side's least gentrified blocks were excluded in the contextual rezoning. Median household incomes for census tracts inside the rezoning's boundaries ranged as high as $51,413. Meanwhile, all of the community board's poorest census tracts, with median incomes as low as $11,963, were left out of the proposal. The plan left out the Lower East Side and East Village's racially diverse waterfront, and did nothing to protect public housing residents.[4] Though white residents made up just 29 percent of Community District 3, 73 percent of the white population was covered by the Bloomberg administration's proposal. And while Asians, Latinos, and blacks made up a broad majority of the population, just 37 percent of the area's Hispanics and 23 percent of its Asian populations were covered by this protective zoning.[5]

# Most of Chinatown and the Lower East Side's least gentrified blocks were excluded in the contextual rezoning.

At public events and in communication with the press, community members argued that the city's proposal was part of a plan to divert development into low-income communities of color. Josephine Lee, an organizer with the Chinese Staff and Workers Association (CSWA), told a reporter:

> It's really blatantly racist, the way they drew their boundaries. The rezoning plan is not so much to protect the East Village as it is to displace the communities of people of color within and around it (Tucker 2008).

Wing Lam, founder of the CSWA, asked rhetorically:

> How can you put a plan like that on the Chinese? Only white [people] like low buildings and sunlight and Chinese don't like low buildings and sunlight? (Anderson et al. 2008).

CSWA and other groups ultimately sued the city, arguing that its Environmental Impact Statement significantly underrepresented the plan's potential displacement of Chinatown's working-class people of color.

In the course of the debates over the rezoning plan, many also questioned why public housing, home to many Asian, Latino and black residents, was excluded from the rezoning. The zoning on these sites had been established decades ago, when gentrification and public housing seemed incompatible. In public forums, some falsely claimed that NYCHA, which was established under state legislation, was exempt from zoning rules. In the end, public housing residents were not included in conversations and plans for the future of their neighborhood.

# Public housing residents were not included in conversations and plans for the future of their neighborhood.

The community board responded to these concerns with enormous hostility. They refused to provide key information to opponents of the plan. The board denied entry to Chinese and Latino members of the public, even when meetings were not full to capacity; at one point, a community board member even shouted at the crowd to "be quiet and stop your Chinese rebellion" (Li 2010).

After a series of blistering hearings, Community Board 3 voted to

**05.C Division Street.**

*Photo: Sarah Friedland, 2016.*

approve the rezoning. In response to the community outcry, the board
also recommended that the city introduce programs to address harassment and eviction of rent regulated tenants, monitor and attempt to halt
demolition of existing buildings in the district, and identify publicly owned
sites for affordable housing. When the plan moved on through the land use
review process to the City Planning Commission, however, all of these recommendations were dropped, and the commission voted to approve the
plan as written (Xu 2013). By the time the plan made it to the city council,
it was virtually assured a victory. Alan Gerson, the city council member
who represented the bulk of Chinatown, called Wing Lam, director of the
Chinese Staff and Workers Association, and asked for his blessing to vote
for the rezoning. A no vote, Gerson argued, would be a useless protest.

When Lam refused to accept this compromise, Gerson offered funding for anti-eviction support work. This suggests that public officials understood that the East Village/Lower East Side rezoning would result in displacement in Chinatown, yet proceeded to support it. On November 19, 2008, the city council voted unanimously to approve the rezoning.

During the public review process, proponents of the rezoning claimed that the plan was too far along to modify. City officials were also firm and sought to placate the opposition with promises that they would support a future rezoning of Chinatown. The city bulldozed ahead.

## THE 2011 SEWARD PARK MIXED-USE DEVELOPMENT PROJECT AND REZONING

The 2008 rezoning affected most of the Lower East Side but excluded one significant area: 20 acres of largely vacant land known as the Seward Park Urban Renewal Area, or SPURA. In 1967, as part of the federal urban renewal program, the city demolished 14 blocks of "blighted" housing and displaced 966 Puerto Rican families, 762 white families, 193 black families, and 178 Chinese families. Eighty percent of them were low-income households (Turner 1984). The city promised to create new housing in place of the "slums" it bulldozed, but instead SPURA languished for decades. The site includes a few isolated public or subsidized housing projects, but the original promise of large-scale low-income housing was never realized. Most of the lots have been used as parking or were fenced off and left vacant.

Over the years there have been both city-led and community-driven proposals to redevelop the site, but they were repeatedly quashed in racially charged political battles. For decades, residents of nearby Cooperative Village, a complex built by and for garment workers — 97.6 percent of whom were white — fought with Chinese, Puerto Rican, and black activists over the site's future (Turner 1984). White leaders, including the long-term New York State Assembly Leader Sheldon Silver, lobbied and maneuvered to ensure that no low-income housing was built on the cleared SPURA land, largely as a way to preserve their enclave and protect their positions of power. Meanwhile, organizations led by and representing working-class people of color fought for public and subsidized housing on the site. They were often promised parcels that were never delivered. The struggle simmered and raged on and off for over 40 years (Buettner 2014).

For decades, residents of nearby Cooperative Village, a complex built by and for garment workers—97.6 percent of whom were white—fought with Chinese, Puerto Rican, and black activists over the site's future.

After the 2008 East Village/Lower East Side rezoning, the city was finally ready to take action on SPURA. Mayor Bloomberg, in concert with Speaker Silver, insisted that any new residential construction on the site be largely "market-rate," with some percentage carved out for lower income tenants. Groups like CSWA and NMASS (National Mobilization Against Sweatshops) rejected this framework. In order to fight the tide of gentrification, and to right the wrongs of the 1967 demolition and displacement, they demanded that this rare tract of publicly owned land be used entirely for low-income housing. The city moved forward with planning and negotiations, often excluding these organizations.

In 2011, the city's plan for SPURA was adopted: about 1,000 apartments would be built, of which 20 percent would be low-income, 20 percent middle-income, and 10 percent senior housing. In their guidelines for development, the city insisted that "the mixed-income character of the neighborhood must be reflected in the development plan for the sites." However, the final plan represents less a picture of Chinatown's current diversity than a model of its gentrified future.

At market rates, 500 of the new apartments would be affordable to less than 1 percent of current Community District 3 residents. Monthly rents in the "affordable" units would be no more than 30 percent of net household income, as per federal and city standards, for those who meet income qualifications. A unit can be considered "affordable" even if it serves persons earning far above the city median income, which is far higher than the neighborhood median income. Thus, among the 500 income-targeted units, at projected rents, 100 units at $3,000 per month would be affordable to only 14 percent of the population in the area; 100 apartments at $2,500 a month would be affordable to 17 percent of the population; and

**118**

300 apartments at $1,000 per month would be affordable to a slim majority (53 percent) of neighborhood residents.

In this vision of a mixed-income neighborhood, less than 1 percent of the population gets half of the housing, half of the apartments go to middle- and upper-middle-income residents, and low wage earners—47 percent of the existing population—cannot afford to live there at all (Chou and Miranda 2011).[6]

In 2015, Sheldon Silver, whose shadow hovered over the site for 40 years, was convicted of massive fraud (unrelated to the project) and forced to resign from the New York State Assembly.

In this vision of a mixed-income neighborhood, half of the apartments go to middle- and upper-middle-income residents, and low wage earners—47 percent of the existing population—cannot afford to live there at all.

## THE IMPACT OF THE REZONINGS: DISPLACEMENT AND LOSS OF AFFORDABLE HOUSING

In 2008 and 2011, when the city's zoning actions took place, Chinatown was already experiencing gentrification pressures, felt most intensely by the neighborhood's Chinese and Latino communities. Since then, the displacement has only persisted and grown.

Between 2008 and 2011, nearly 6,000 existing and newly developed neighborhood apartments became unaffordable to households making middle-class wages.[7] In 2010, median rents for newcomers to the neighborhood were $1,762, a third higher than the citywide figure.[8] By 2014,

**05.D** The Coalition to Protect Chinatown and The Lower East Side and its supporters march to City Hall demanding passage of the Chinatown Working Group community plan.

Photo: Samuel Stein, 2016.

median asking rents had reached $3,000 a month (Furman Center 2014). Much of this change is due to the deregulation of rent-stabilized apartments, which are disappearing through both legal inaction and illegal transformations at a rapid rate.

The prospect of rising rents, according to then-Democratic District Leader Paul Newell, "gives [landords] the incentive to have short-term residents—to flip people in-and-out" who pay more and are less likely to challenge deteriorating conditions (Barbino 2011). This, in turn, encourages landlords to harass long-term or low rent paying residents. As one community organizer told reporters in 2011: "Pretty much every day we have someone coming to us with a new story of a landlord harassing them" (Barbino 2011).

As rents rose, income disparities expanded. Average incomes for white residents in the neighborhood took off from $35,504 in 2000 to $58,265 in 2010. Meanwhile, wages did not keep up for people of color. Average incomes for Asian Chinatown residents actually decreased between 2000 and 2010, from $31,368 to $29,524. One-third of Asians in Chinatown live below the poverty line.

## 05.E Loss of Latino, Asian, and Black Populations, Growth of White Population in Chinatown and the Lower East Side, 2000–2010

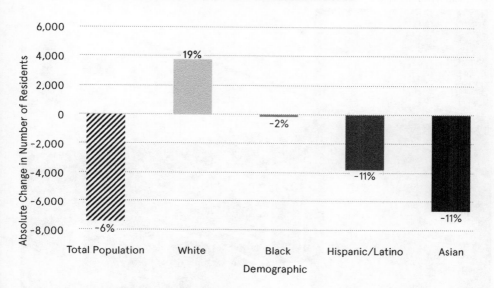

*Percentages represent the percent change in number of residents within a demographic between 2000 and 2010.

Asian American Legal Defense and Education Fund, Chinatown Then and Now: Gentrification in Boston, New York, and Philadelphia, 2013, p.29 www.aaldef.org/

Between 2000 and 2010, according to an analysis of U.S. Census data by the Asian American Legal Defense and Education Fund, the number of residents of color drastically declined, with a loss of 6,707 Asian residents, 3,823 Latinos, and 131 black residents, while the white population increased by 3,785 residents.

This widespread gentrification and displacement of people of color is directly linked to the city's zoning actions: when landowners find that rezoning has increased the potential value of their land, they typically sell the property for upscale redevelopment, or employ legal and illegal tactics to remove low-income tenants and charge higher rents. If Chinatown had been included in the rezoning with zoning designations that protected existing buildings, the pressures of gentrification and displacement could have been minimized.

**05.F  A new hotel in Chinatown built after the 2008 rezoning.**

*Photo: Sarah Friedland, 2016.*

# NEW LUXURY DEVELOPMENT

In the absence of zoning protections, Chinatown has experienced a rash of new upscale construction. A 2008 survey found 26 new luxury buildings in Chinatown; since then dozens more have been built (CAAAV 2008). These new buildings are easily identifiable: on the whole, they are taller and wider than most Chinatown buildings, they lack affordable retail spaces, and they tend to feature sheets of reflective glass or protruding balconies. Chinatown realtors are not shy about the people they are looking to attract. One agent marketing 123 Baxter, a new luxury building that claims to be in "SoHo South," told a real estate newspaper she was looking for tenants who are "young and come from a lot of money" (Weiman 2007). The same realtor told *The New York Times* that their target was people "who want luxury but want to stay under the radar and who think SoHo is too trendy already—I think trust-fund babies with ripped jeans is the profile we're looking at" (Toy 2006).

Hotels are also rising throughout Chinatown. They are typically discouraged in residential neighborhoods, but permitted under Chinatown's zoning. On blocks zoned for manufacturing, hotels can be built as of right.

Now that Chinatown is no longer a garment-manufacturing hub, many of the spaces that once housed sweatshops are being converted into luxury hotels or demolished for new hotel construction (Kwong and Stein 2015). These properties include:

- At 54 Canal Street, DLJ RE Capital Partners, an investment firm with developments in the US and China, is working on a 140-room conversion.
- On 154 Madison, a new Comfort Inn squeezed into a slender lot.
- On 185 Bowery, Brack Capital, a Dutch real estate conglomerate with properties around the world, is opening "CitizenM Downtown," a new 300-room hotel that is larger than its Times Square counterpart.
- At 50 Bowery, Alex Chu of Eastbank is demolishing the old Silver Palace restaurant, site of one of the longest and most militant labor strikes in Chinatown's history, and building a 22-story hotel.

These developments will do nothing for Chinatown's existing population, and will only advance the neighborhood's transformation into a tourist attraction along the lines of the 1950s "China Village" plan.

## 05.G Development in Chinatown.

*Photo: Sarah Friedland, 2016.*

# ADDING INSULT TO INJURY: THE EXTELL BUILDING

One of the most alarming new developments is a proposed 80-story, 800-unit super luxury apartment building along the waterfront in Chinatown. Until recently, it was the site of a 24-hour Pathmark, the only accessible supermarket for the neighborhood's low-income population. On March 15, 2013, Extell Development Company purchased the land for over $103 million. Since Pathmark had 30 years left on its lease, Extell also bought out their lease for an additional $46 million, bringing the total acquisition price to just under $150 million.

The new building will feature such absurdist amenities as a golf simulator room, a dog spa, and a cigar room, and is designed as a virtual gated community. The developer, however, is financing their project with public money (including Low Income Housing Tax Credits and 421-a tax abatements), and is building a separate, smaller, lower quality building with below-market rents. The plan is to build a 13-story, 205-apartment structure next to the high-rise, for families making up to 60 percent of New York's Area Median Income. A qualifying family of four could earn up to $51,540 (Litvak 2014) while the median income for that particular census block is just $20,450 (Pratt Center for Community Development et al. 2013). This segregated development will exclude people of color and low-income families currently living in the area, while also creating secondary displacement pressures by fueling rising rents and land prices.

# DISPLACEMENT OF PUBLIC HOUSING RESIDENTS

Luxury development has also been proposed on the neighborhood's public housing campuses, which were also excluded from 2008's contextual rezoning. Smith, LaGuardia, and Baruch houses were chosen as potential development sites in a 2013 proposal for infill development at eight Manhattan public housing projects. The new buildings would be placed either on parking lots or on land now used for parks and playgrounds. At Smith Houses, plans were released for one 50-story luxury building (with 20 percent "affordable" housing), which would tower 33 stories over the current buildings, and two 35-story buildings, including one on top of the project's baseball field (Smith 2013). Smith resident leader Aixa Torres told reporters: "They're going to literally squeeze my residents like they're roaches and they're going to build this huge beautiful complex" (Smith 2013).

**124**

While Mayor Michael Bloomberg's infill proposal was defeated by resi-dent organizing, NYCHA (the New York City Housing Authority) has sold and leased property for private development on a piecemeal basis through-out the city, and is planning a new iteration of the large-scale infill plan. Since 2013, NYCHA has sold 54 plots (441 square feet) to private develop-ers (Smith 2015). In 2015, Mayor de Blasio proposed the "NextGeneration" plan for NYCHA; activists were quick to dub it "NextGentrification" (Pinto 2015). The plan's centerpiece was a proposal to lease large amounts of NYCHA land to private developers, who would build 7,500 new units of housing at 50 percent market rate and 50 percent "affordable," though even these income levels would be significantly higher than public housing averages (Nahmias 2015). The plan also included steps towards privatizing select developments and increasing rent collection levels, with the implied threat of evictions for non-payment (Navarro 2015). Many fear that these actions, undeterred by zoning changes, are creating a pathway to privat-ization and laying claim to one of the last guarantees of affordable housing for low-income people of color in Chinatown and beyond.

## EXACERBATING INEQUALITIES

By restricting development in the more affluent East Village and push-ing development demand further into Chinatown, and by rezoning SPURA to stimulate high-end construction, the city's land use policies have in-creased displacement pressures on the Asian, Latino, and black popula-tions of Chinatown and the Lower East Side.

The real-life impacts of displacement go far beyond losing one's home. Many tenants face constant landlord harassment, rising rents, and deteri-orating conditions. Residents of aging tenement buildings frequently con-front landlord negligence, often a form of harassment, that results in leaks and mold, chipping paint and plaster, vermin infestations, and more seri-ous structural deterioration. Many of these low-income tenants are paying upwards of 50 percent of their incomes to live in such hazardous and in-humane conditions, often while facing housing court battles and off-the-record conflicts. Most recently, in May 2015, Chinatown tenants brought these issues to light in a protest of a local slumlord. Tenants and activists described living conditions:

> rats [are] all over the place coming out from the holes. [Tenants] have to knock on the door to make the rats leave before they can even enter their own bath-room (Airoldi 2015).

One resident has to hold an umbrella when she uses the restroom to protect herself from leaks. As David Tieu of the National Mobilization Against Sweatshops stated:

> A lot of luxury development has been pushed into our community [...] and it encourages landlords [...] to use these slumlord tactics to push out long-time residents (Airoldi 2015).

A 2010 tenant lawsuit claimed that landlord harassment tactics included:

> disrupting three tenant meetings by calling the police; rejecting rent payments; frivolously pursuing legal eviction proceedings; suspending essential services for a prolonged period of time; and ordering tenants to remove Chinese cultural symbols and decorations from their doors (Lee 2009).

Residential and commercial displacement is particularly impactful in immigrant communities, where locally run businesses and organizations serve particular linguistic and cultural needs. These losses of community and culture are both emotional and practical. As Chinatown and the Lower East Side's Asian and Latino residents, stores, and cultural centers are displaced by new development and rising rents, those who are able to stay lose local resources and are increasingly isolated. As their communities shrink, they are increasingly underrepresented and underserved.

# Residential and commercial displacement is particularly impactful in immigrant communities, where locally run businesses and organizations serve particular linguistic and cultural needs.

# THE COMMUNITY PLAN
# FOR CHINATOWN:
# HOW THE CITY DESTROYED
# THE EQUITABLE ALTERNATIVE

One way to curb displacement and segregation is to engage in and implement genuine community planning, which can manage development and
protect existing residents and businesses. After Chinatown was excluded
from the 2008 rezoning, the three community boards that contain piec-
es of Chinatown—Manhattan's community boards 1, 2, and 3—came together with over 40 neighborhood organizations to form the Chinatown
Working Group, a body tasked with creating a planning and zoning doc-
ument that would help shape Chinatown's future. Rather than creating a
formal 197-a plan, a slow and cumbersome process that ends in a legally
non-binding plan, the Chinatown Working Group aimed to build internal
consensus, then hire an outside consultant to turn their ideas into a formal rezoning proposal.

In consultation with DCP and other agencies, planners from the Pratt
Institute developed a formal plan, which included a special zoning district, strict anti-eviction and anti-harassment provisions, a very targeted

**05.H  The Plan for Chinatown and Surrounding Areas:**
**Preserving Affordability and Authenticity**

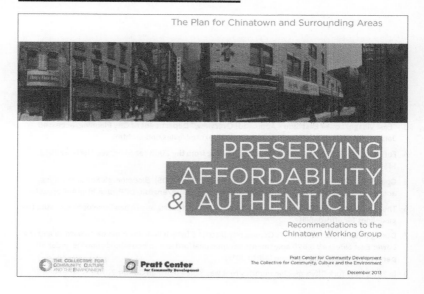

The Plan for Chinatown and Surrounding Areas

PRESERVING
AFFORDABILITY
& AUTHENTICITY

Recommendations to the
Chinatown Working Group

THE COLLECTIVE FOR
COMMUNITY, CULTURE
AND THE ENVIRONMENT

Pratt Center
for Community Development

Pratt Center for Community Development
The Collective for Community, Culture and the Environment

December 2013

and comparatively affordable inclusionary zoning program, restrictions on big box stores and hotels, and more allowances for light manufacturing in character with the neighborhood's existing economic activity.

As the plan was being approved by Community Board 3, however, DCP Director Carl Weisbrod sent a letter to the board, informing them that they had no intention to approve the Chinatown Working Group's plan. Calling it too ambitious, they offered to consider the portions of the plan that emphasized development over preservation (Litvak 2015). This suggests that the problems of racially unequal zoning practices were not limited to the Bloomberg administration, but constitute a pattern and practice of discriminatory planning policies, deeply imbedded in city government. In response, Chinatown and Lower East Side residents and workers have been protesting the mayor and his planning priorities at the Extell development site, at city hall, at Gracie Mansion, and at real estate banquets. With their own community plan in hand, Chinatown activists are demanding an end to racist rezonings, and the beginning of a new era of community planning.

**Endnotes**

1. The author would like to thank Wendy Chang, Kai Wen Yang, Gui Yang, Wing Lam (Chinese Staff and Workers Association), and David Tieu (National Mobilization Against Sweatshops) for all their input and guidance, and recognize Peter Kwong for his many years of mentorship and insightful analysis.

2. *Chinese Staff and Workers Association et al., Appellants, v. City of New York et al., Respondents.* Court of Appeals of the State of New York. Decided November 18, 1986. 68 N.Y.2d 359 (1986).

3. "East Village/Lower East Side - Approved! Overview," Department of City Planning, accessed January 23, 2016, http://www.nyc.gov/html/dcp/html/evles/index.shtml.

4. For more on the exclusion of most public housing from the 2008 rezoning, see Martinez 2010, 143–145.

5. Coalition to Protect Chinatown and the Lower East Side (2008), *Bloomberg's Racist Rezoning*, accessed May 4, 2014. http://protectchinatownandles.org/english/DCP_plan.html#affordable.

6. These calculations assume the federal Department of Housing and Urban Development's standard guidelines for affordability.

7. During this period, Manhattan's Community District 3 (which includes most of Chinatown and the Lower East Side) saw 5,890 apartments become unaffordable to households making under 80 percent of Area Median Income (ANHD 2013).

8. In 2010, New York City's median monthly rent was $1,184 (Furman Center 2011).

# CHAPTER SIX

# ALTERNATIVES: COMMUNITY-BASED PLANNING AND HOUSING IN THE PUBLIC DOMAIN

TOM ANGOTTI

New York City must change the way it deals with land use, zoning, and housing. We must find better solutions that preserve viable neighborhoods, promote development, and improve the quality of life for all residents, while at the same time addressing the issues of economic and racial equality and fair housing. Land use planning can be a platform from which government promotes inclusive neighborhood improvement without displacing low-income people and people of color.

Before doing anything else, the city's political leadership and those who run the city's planning and housing agencies must openly acknowledge that race matters. They must not confuse the rich diversity that has always characterized the city's population with the racial segregation and displacement that have been part of the city's long history. They need to examine how city policies promote racial exclusion and displacement. This must become an open public discussion and there should be no tolerance for the claim that planning and zoning are "race-neutral."

Strong voices in neighborhoods, like East New York, the South Bronx, and East Harlem, are now confronting and rejecting rezoning proposals and calling for better solutions. Activists are demanding that before any community gets rezoned there should be serious long-term planning. Not improvised focus groups and random brainstorming sessions, which the

**06. A Protestors at Hands Across Harlem, an event organized by the Coalition to Save Harlem, in front of the Adam Clayton Powell Jr. State Office Building. April 12, 2008.**

*Photo: Rezoning Harlem. Film. Directed by Natasha Florentino and Tamara Gubernat. New York: Third World News Reel, 2008.*

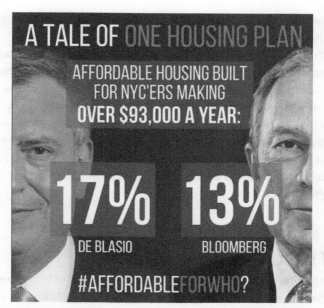

**06.B** Real Affordability for All, a coalition of over 50 grassroots groups, has criticized the de Blasio and Bloomberg affordable housing programs for skewing benefits towards higher income groups. However, they do not question the program's promotion of market-rate development as a pre-condition for affordable housing.

*Photo: Real Affordability for All, 2016 .*

city has so far promoted. Not charrettes or charades that result in giant wish lists that are then followed by a rezoning cooked up in advance by the Department of City Planning (DCP). Not promises for community benefits that may never materialize, but fundamental changes in the ways that city agencies think and act when dealing with the city's diverse communities.

Zoning by itself cannot address the critical challenges of homelessness, lack of affordable housing, sea-level rise and climate change, the aging mass transit system, unsafe streets, the epidemics of asthma and obesity, lack of open space and recreational opportunities, the proliferation of unhealthy food, overcrowded and segregated schools, and a waste management system that does not reduce waste but only takes it somewhere else. Zoning has played a minor role in abetting environmental injustices, but by itself zoning cannot end racial discrimination and segregation. And this is only a short list of things that zoning can and cannot do! Still, zoning matters because, in combination with other city policies and private actions, it can mean a drastic transformation of our neighborhoods leading to the displacement of people of color.

With leadership from its elected leaders, New York City can take the first step by changing the mission of DCP from the care and maintenance of the Zoning Resolution to planning. Long-term, comprehensive planning at different scales: citywide, neighborhood, and regional. Top-down and bottom-up planning. Planning that addresses in an integrated way the everyday problems and issues confronting people who live and work in the city and those who visit. This fundamental shift, if it is to be meaningful, will require changes in the way the rest of government functions and relates to neighborhoods.

# NO MORE ZONING WITHOUT PLANNING

Planning by itself is no more the solution than is zoning, but this is no excuse for continuing to zone without a plan, or for failing to plan. As we have shown, zoning without a plan leaves the future in the hands of a small group of landowners, lawyers, and experts and undermines efforts to develop equitable, feasible strategies for community preservation and development. New York City is the only major city in the United States that has never prepared and approved a long-term plan. As a result, it has spent a century zoning without a plan—without a clear vision of the city's long-term future. It has been regulating the built environment through zoning without integrating the decisions it makes with the everyday lives of people who live and work in the city, nor has it tried to project visions for the social and economic well-being of the city that promote fundamental principles of social and racial equality.

Planning is not some empty abstraction out of a textbook. It is the democratic process of conceiving a better world at all levels—the block, the neighborhood, city, region, nation, and world. It should help us to solve our current problems while at the same time dealing with future challenges. Planning should seek to bring to the fore the diverse and often conflicting policy objectives arising from communities and from within government. It should require us to confront these conflicts and contradictions and look squarely at the long-range future of our communities, the city, and region. Planning should come before and after zoning, and zoning should be put where it belongs—in a large toolbox with a whole array of instruments that can be used to shape the future of the city. The toolbox must include the city's operating and capital budgets, agency policies and practices, and all government practices as they affect neighborhoods.

Planning takes time. It can (and usually should) be slow. The city needs to allocate the time to plan and also set reasonable limits. The city at all levels has individuals and groups that disagree with one another. Planning will not make these disagreements disappear. But once there is agreement on long-term strategies and specific proposals, it can actually save time even if it cannot resolve all differences.

All of this by itself is not radical thinking. The American Planning Association says: "When government officials, business leaders, and citizens come together to build communities that enrich people's lives, that's planning." Planners Network, an association of professional planners, academics, and activists, goes deeper and says, "planning should be a tool for allocating resources and developing the environment to eliminate the great inequalities of wealth and power in our society." Planners have always differed when it comes to defining their mission, but the one thing they agree on is that planning is both valuable and essential for consciously shaping the future of our living environments.[1]

According to the Code of Ethics and Professional Conduct of the American Planning Association and American Institute of Certified Planners, its members should "seek social justice by working to expand choice and opportunity for all persons, recognizing a special responsibility to plan for the needs of the disadvantaged and to promote racial and economic integration." Peter Marcuse, emeritus professor of Urban Planning at Columbia University, believes that this statement is overly vague and lacking in enforcement measures (Marcuse 2014). However, in New York City, this minimal principle is not observed or even a matter for open discussion and debate. The first step must be to open up the discussion about planning to "seek social justice" and "promote racial and economic integration."

We are not talking about simply creating a new city office or hiring some more professionals. There must be a fundamental shift in the culture and practice of the Department of City Planning, from top to bottom, towards real planning at multiple scales—from the block up to the neighborhood, city, and regional levels—and away from the exclusive use of zoning in land use policy. Of course, one city agency alone can never do all the planning or solve all problems, but according to the New York City Charter, it is the responsibility of the DCP to take the lead within government when it comes to planning for the long-term future of the city. The city's planners must be the advocates of planning at city hall and with other agencies, and not just the technocrats in charge of zoning regulations.

"There must be a fundamental shift in the culture and practice of the Department of City Planning, from top to bottom, towards real planning at multiple scales—from the block up to the neighborhood, city, and regional levels—and away from the exclusive use of zoning in land use policy."

It may seem contradictory, but for community-based planning dedicated to economic and racial equity to work, it requires citywide planning that is also dedicated to the same principles. We are talking about real top-down planning and real community-based planning. The two can and should coexist and the planning process should manage both the conflict and cooperation that is inevitably part of this coexistence and is essential to our active civic life. Both should be held accountable to basic principles of social equality and racial justice.

## ZONING CANNOT SOLVE THE HOUSING PROBLEM

One of the most disingenuous elements in the city's current planning practice is the one that claims to address housing issues through the use of zoning powers. Inclusionary zoning, which establishes requirements that a proportion of new development be affordable housing, is a good idea in principle, and has been partially successful in some places (Calavita and Mallach 2010), but it is not by itself a solution to the lack of affordable housing and, as we have seen in the cases of Williamsburg, Harlem, and Chinatown, can contribute to the displacement of more affordable housing than it creates. Mayor de Blasio's recently approved Mandatory

Inclusionary Housing (MIH) program mandates that around 25 percent of all new housing in newly rezoned areas be affordable.

However, even if successful, MIH will not prevent the displacement of communities of color and, as we have seen, the new "affordable" units are hardly affordable to most existing residents in communities of color. It will mean that almost all new development—as much as 80% of new housing units—will be market-rate housing which in turn increases rents and housing prices and displaces more affordable housing units than it creates. Preliminary estimates are that MIH might create only a small fraction of the 200,000 affordable units promised in the mayor's housing plan. The most serious problem is that, in practice, MIH will be used as a Trojan Horse to convince communities to accept rezoning schemes that will result in substantial new market-rate housing and significant displacement.

In practice, Mandatory Inclusionary Housing will be used as a Trojan Horse to convince communities to accept rezoning schemes that will result in substantial new market-rate housing and significant displacement.

## NO MORE AFFORDABLE HOUSING SCAMS!

In general, zoning changes are a very weak tool for promoting housing development. Zoning is a regulatory tool; the basic tools for housing development are financing and land, and zoning by itself won't produce either. Zoning changes frequently increase the cost of land, which in turn increases the cost of housing. If the city upzones to encourage private development, that will invariably produce the most expensive housing, which itself will trigger rising land costs and rents in surrounding areas, placing the housing out of reach to people with low incomes. Inclusionary zoning can lead to the creation of some low- and moderate-income housing in areas with high land costs, but does not work well elsewhere. If the city mandates that a portion of new housing be "affordable," government may still provide incentives and subsidies that will help pay for it, in which case it is the public funding that is critical and not the zoning (and those funds would likely go further if invested in more moderately priced areas). Clearly, zoning by itself will not do the trick.

As we showed in Chapter One, new market-rate development, whether or not it is stimulated by a rezoning, has resulted in the loss of more affordable housing units than it has created. Inclusionary zoning has not worked very well and making it mandatory, though a step forward, will not help when the affordable units created are not affordable to most community residents. The result will be displacement, and that will have a racial edge.

# THE DEATH AND LIFE OF COMMUNITY-BASED PLANNING IN NEW YORK CITY

In response to calls from the neighborhoods for real planning before any zoning changes, the de Blasio administration has encouraged and supported what it calls community-based planning. These plans have been promoted in East New York, the South Bronx, and East Harlem, neighborhoods slated for rezonings by DCP. Aided by foundation-funded non-profit groups and allies, the planners organize focus groups and visioning sessions that encourage residents to talk about their concerns and make proposals. They involve under-staffed community boards and staff from local community and cultural institutions. The proposals that arise are dutifully noted. This process may take weeks, months, or even a year or more. It results in a written report with attractive graphics and a list of proposals. In the end, however, it is not legally binding on anyone and will join the list of community-based plans that were shelved and ignored. What will inevitably follow is a rezoning proposal that advances the predictable formulas used by the zoning technocrats at DCP (as we explained in Chapter One).

These planning charades may generate a long wish list of potential projects, including some "affordable" housing and promises of future capital expenditures, all of which can, sooner or later, be forgotten. Such a fate is not inevitable but has most often been the result in the past. The 2005 Williamsburg rezoning, for example, was accompanied by a lengthy

**136**

memorandum, signed by the deputy mayor, promising many community benefits that, in the long run, proved impossible to get. In sum, what passes for planning in New York City is at best a Faustian bargain between community representatives and city officials that allows an unpopular zoning change to move forward.

The planning charades may generate a long wish list of potential projects, including some "affordable" housing and promises of future capital expenditures, all of which can, sooner or later, be forgotten.

The problem starts with the official myth that invariably emanates from city hall and DCP: new development is going to occur no matter what, so you had better figure out what you can get out of it, from either the city or the developers. This is an invitation to either lie under the bulldozer and get run over or get out of its way. It assumes that you have no power, no prospect of control over the future of your community. It is an invitation to make a backroom deal that leaves you with some token benefit. It requires that you forget the long history of community resistance like the civil rights struggles against the urban renewal bulldozers. It ignores the long history of exclusionary, NIMBY ("Not in My Backyard") practices by white and wealthy neighborhoods, which have done quite well stopping new development they did not like, with or without a plan. These neighborhoods know that nothing is inevitable as long as they use their political power and resources to insure that it goes their way. The planners in government need to insure that the same standards apply in all neighborhoods. They need to stop making phony predictions of inevitable change and seriously consider the racial bias involved when communities of color are urged to accommodate themselves to what they are told is the inevitable.

The problem starts with the official myth that invariably emanates from city hall and DCP: new development is going to occur no matter what, so you had better figure out what you can get out of it, from either the city or the developers. This is an invitation to either lie under the bulldozer and get run over or get out of its way.

Another myth promoted by the planners is that community-based planning is potentially dangerous because all communities are inevitably exclusionary—proponents of NIMBY. If communities gain control over future land use, they claim, they will stop all development. The persistence of exclusionary, mostly white, low-density enclaves in the city points us toward more persistent exclusionary practices that might pass for community planning, but have nothing to do with inclusive, progressive community planning. On the other hand, there is a strong track record of inclusive community-based planning in New York City and many community plans have been built on principles of environmental justice and social inclusion.

## COMMUNITY BOARDS AND ULURP: FIRST STEPS TOWARDS COMMUNITY-BASED PLANNING

Mayor John Lindsay introduced community planning boards in the 1960s in response to growing neighborhood activism, most notably the firm opposition to urban renewal and displacement of minority communities.

As community organizing accelerated in opposition to the city's plans, the city's civic elite, wary of giving neighborhoods too much power, fashioned a proposal that created the Uniform Land Use Review Procedure (ULURP), and 59 community districts, each with a community board. Since 1975, all zoning changes have been reviewed and voted on by a community board as well as the CPC, borough president, and city council.

Since they first appeared, however, community boards have struggled to be relevant players in the decision-making process. Board members are unpaid and appointed by borough presidents and city council members. The total administrative budget for all 59 community boards is less than .01 percent of the city's budget, and even though the 1989 charter reform called for each board to have its own professional planner, the city has skirted this requirement. Community boards can influence major decisions in a variety of ways but they have very little leverage even though their communities are directly affected by land use changes. They are constantly reminded that their vote is "only advisory," a phrase that translates into "irrelevant" and encourages a fatalistic acceptance of what they are told is inevitable.

City officials and developers who know how to work the ULURP process often engage in a cynical game that points to the sometimes emotional and disorderly public hearings at community boards and other public hearings as proof that giving the boards more power would be an invitation to chaos and NIMBY politics. This finger pointing allows the most powerful players to reserve the real power for themselves and cuts off the calls for the city to give the boards more power and resources.

The first order of business in the promotion of community planning is to end this dysfunctional structure of decision-making. While ULURP may be relatively efficient for developers and city staff because the process is time-limited, it does not require that the decisions that are made be based on and consistent with comprehensive community-based plans. Community boards remain mere pawns whose best shot at influence is to vote in favor or against actions with conditions, with the hope that the City Planning Commission and city council might agree with them.

It is time for another major revision to the New York City Charter that empowers community boards and, most importantly, holds them accountable to principles of social justice—the same principles to which the higher levels of government must be held accountable. Too many community boards in white neighborhoods openly discriminate on the basis of race and ethnicity and fail to involve all parts of their neighborhoods; a charter revision and constant oversight are necessary as remedies. All of this will not work unless the city's budget guarantees that all boards have the resources needed to become responsible and truly representative partners in government (Angotti 2010).

It is time for another major revision to the New York City Charter that empowers community boards and, most importantly, holds them accountable to principles of social justice—the same principles to which the higher levels of government must be held accountable.

## WHO KILLED THE 197-A PLANS?

Community-based planning in New York City is not a pipe dream. Over the last half-century, more than 100 community plans were developed in the city. Many of these were alternatives to private or public projects that would have displaced people (Municipal Art Society n.d.; 1998). Many came out of the civil rights and environmental justice movements, included proposals for housing development, and endorsed zoning measures that would favor low-income and affordable housing (Angotti 2008).

Community-based planning in New York City has had a powerful link with the movements for civil rights and environmental justice. The 1989 reform of the New York City Charter was a product of a major civil rights lawsuit against the city that eliminated the Board of Estimate as the major decision-making body in the city because it gave disproportionate power to boroughs with larger white populations and was thus in violation of the Equal Protection clause of the United States Constitution. Community activists, including those who had opposed urban renewal and the displacement of low-income minorities, wanted the charter to guarantee a more powerful role for communities. The only thing they got, however, was an explicit affirmation in the charter that community boards could prepare their own plans, under Section 197-a of the city charter, and present them to the borough president, CPC, and city council for approval, a promise that the city would review ULURP proposals for some new infrastructure to determine whether the community affected would have more than its "fair share" of burdensome facilities, and a promise that the 59 community boards would have their own professional planner (Angotti 1997; 2008, 113–177).

To date only 13 plans have been officially approved as "197-a plans." Significantly, most of the community plans emerged from communities of color and were not initiated by government. No community board has yet to receive funds to hire a planner. Significantly, less than two decades after the charter reform the wave of new community plans has subsided because of the way that DCP has undermined the process and ignored the community plans after they are approved. The last 197-a plan was approved in 2009.

The Campaign for Community-Based Planning, a group of community activists and professionals, spent a decade trying to get city government to take community planning seriously, and then gave up. Instead of promoting community planning the city launched the largest rezoning blitz in its history; while it paid lip service to community-based planning the city deployed Madison Avenue techniques in neighborhoods targeted for rezoning and gave the impression that all voices were being heard.

The Williamsburg case (Chapter Three) is the most dramatic example of how the city has undermined community-based 197-a plans; the community had reached consensus on development priorities after more than a decade of debate and discussion. The DCP-initiated zoning change effectively killed the approved community plan and sent a message to other communities that the 197-a process is not worth the effort. In Harlem (Chapter Four) a community plan for Manhattanville served as cover for a sweeping rezoning to promote the expansion of Columbia University. The Chinatown case (Chapter Five) is another dramatic example; DCP summarily rejected a community rezoning plan that the city itself had encouraged. There are no community plans in the 197-a pipeline today.

While community planning emerged from community resistance to displacement and racial bias, DCP has been quite skillful at channeling its own resistance to community planning. DCP established narrow guidelines for 197-a plans that privilege land use over all other issues and fail to address questions of social equality and environmental justice. DCP's Rules for the Processing of Plans Pursuant to Charter Section 197-a also outlines a lengthy and cumbersome process for preparing and approving 197-a plans, yet another disincentive for volunteer boards with limited staff support. At the same time DCP bogs down community plans, it maintains its own priority of focusing on zoning.

# While community planning emerged from community resistance to displacement and racial bias, DCP has been quite skillful at channeling its own resistance to community planning.

The roadblocks to community-based planning have a class and racial edge since the wealthier and whiter community boards can more easily raise funds, recruit volunteer professionals, and use their political influence to pass both 197-a and zoning plans. This is what happened in Riverdale, the wealthiest and whitest community in the Bronx. The community board there had their 197-a plan approved in 2003 and within two years DCP gave them all the rezonings they asked for, including a Special Natural Area District that protected green space from development (Angotti 2008, 180–181). Contrast this with working class Williamsburg, which took over a decade to do its plan, only to have the city force through its own massive rezoning plan that undermined the basic principles of the community's 197-a plan. Or Chinatown, which spent seven years doing a plan that was summarily rejected by DCP.

Community-based planning is a means by which New Yorkers can exercise their democratic right to participate in making the decisions that affect the communities where they live and work. That right has been unequally distributed and low-income communities of color have not received their fair share. There are no recipes or formulas for community planning but the first step is to fundamentally alter the relationship

**142**

between city government and its neighborhoods. Community boards must have stronger powers and more resources. DCP must start planning at multiple scales. The planning process needs to be connected to the city's capital and operating budgets so plans have concrete results. City agencies have to be held accountable to neighborhoods. All of this may require another change to the city charter that re-balances the distribution of power away from a top-down system with a strong mayor who oversees powerful agencies, while the more than eight million residents of the city only get to deal with the weaker city council and even weaker community boards.

Giving more power to community boards alone is not enough. Too many white community boards have been allowed to use their informal powers to exclude minorities. Too many community boards have no representation across generations, ethnicities, gender and sexual orientation. Too many have not been monitored or held accountable to basic principles of democratic governance and inclusion.

We can learn from former Rochester Mayor William A. Johnson, Jr., a civil rights advocate and African American who headed the Urban League of Rochester for 21 years before becoming mayor. He invited neighborhoods to develop their own plans and budget priorities. According to Johnson:

> Most mayors like to think they're the most important person in the city. Most elected officials are threatened by anything they can't control. And citizen-based planning can be unpredictable, messy and very difficult to control. When urban renewal inevitably failed, people in damaged neighborhoods were expected to pull themselves up by their bootstraps. This is hardly the way to inspire people [...] We believe that a community must always remain a matter of face-to-face interaction. That this idea can seem radical in America is, to me, a sign of how much we view people as objects, not the subjects, of community.

> In Rochester, we have a proud tradition of vigorous debate, followed by meaningful action. We have a tradition of taking the path less traveled. Frederick Douglass and Susan B. Anthony [who lived in Rochester] wouldn't have gotten anywhere if they kept their mouths shut or stayed put in their living rooms (Johnson 2001).

# DEALING WITH DISPLACEMENT: HOUSING IN THE PUBLIC DOMAIN

Just as going "back to the future" of grassroots democracy can help undo an unjust system of land use controls, we can look to the past for answers to the disappearance of affordable housing in communities of color. New

York City has perhaps the largest array of affordable housing programs of any municipality in the United States. However, the city has followed the lead of federal and state governments since the 1980s as they moved away from housing for low-income working people towards the vaguely defined "affordable housing" serving mostly middle-income households.

Too much of this new housing is targeted to the middle, too much is not permanently affordable, and too much is feeding the process of gentrification and displacement. Since the 1980s, the city's "affordable" housing was designed as a public-private partnership that would land the housing units developed and improved with city financing back in the private marketplace, where the owners would then benefit from increases in land values. Many individual owners have indeed benefited, but these were not necessarily the people who needed housing the most, and many of the housing units are no longer affordable.

There has been one exception to this rule. The New York City Housing Authority (NYCHA) was the first major authority in the nation and is still the largest. It houses over 400,000 people today, more than any other housing program in the city and is the largest housing authority in the nation. It is home to many of the people who need housing the most, including working people and city employees who would otherwise be forced to live in the dwindling stock of privately owned low-rent housing. While the majority of residents are people of color, public housing tenants are truly a rainbow of races and ethnicities. Until the federal government began draconian budget cuts, and state and city governments also withdrew their support, NYCHA was what one scholar called "public housing that worked" (Dagen Bloom 2008).

The current status of NYCHA is dire because of its lack of funding (Angotti and Morse 2014; Community Service Society 2015). However, instead of stepping up and restoring the necessary funds, city government has once again adopted a mantra of inevitability, basically claiming that the only way to save public housing is to bring in the private sector. This is reminiscent of the rationale behind the federal urban renewal program: the only way to save the community is to move it out and bring in private investment. However, the "inevitable" lack of funds could easily dissipate if there were appropriations from government—in the same way that the city and state are stepping in (at least minimally) to save the mass transit system. If the federal government alone could take what it spends on a single new aircraft carrier, NYCHA's capital deficit would disappear overnight. The end of public housing is not inevitable.

Instead of wiping the slate clean and getting rid of NYCHA, the city has begun to transform public housing into a public-private partnership, in which the private partner is bound to wield superior power. The NYCHA administration is already thinking like a developer and not like the custodian of a public good. In its current plan (City of New York 2015), the agency speaks of its "portfolio" instead of its obligations as custodian of a public trust. Instead of open spaces, basketball courts, and parking areas in NYCHA complexes, it sees "underutilized" sites ripe for development. It proposes building 10,000 new "affordable" housing units on NYCHA "property."

# The city has begun to transform public housing into a public-private partnership, in which the private partner is bound to wield superior power.

After tenants and civic groups rallied to stop the Bloomberg infill plan to build luxury housing at eight NYCHA projects in Manhattan, the de Blasio administration offered a plan just as ambitious. It would lease authority land throughout the city through partnerships with private and non-profit developers. The process of partial privatization is underway. It can and should be reversed for two compelling reasons: public housing is the most cost-effective way of providing permanently affordable housing, and since it is publicly owned, it is much easier for the city to promote fair housing goals than it is in the private market.

Public housing is cost-effective because capital costs are paid up front and not passed on to residents in the form of mortgage debt; economies of scale allow for savings in operation and maintenance. Also, relief from the property tax benefits the low-income households who need it the most (unlike the billions in 421-a and J-51 exemptions that go to luxury housing developers). If the city, state, and federal governments were to commit capital funds to both save public housing and create new housing for low-income people in neighborhoods facing gentrification and displacement, they could save tax dollars and neighborhoods, and move one step closer to a more equitable and racially integrated city.

If the city, state, and federal governments were to commit capital funds to both save public housing and create new housing for low-income people in neighborhoods facing gentrification and displacement, they could save tax dollars and neighborhoods, and move one step closer to a more equitable and racially integrated city.

Most of the hundreds of thousands of new affordable housing units created by the city are in programs where the affordability expires in relatively short periods of time. One positive step forward is that under the MIH program all affordable units must remain permanently affordable. However, these units will represent a very small percentage of all units. Also, we do not know how these programs fuel gentrification and displacement because the city fails to track the units, their occupants, and the surrounding neighborhoods over the long term. Many of them simply disappear into "the market." It is time that the city begin monitoring the incomes and racial composition of those who benefit from its housing programs so that it can take affirmative measures to insure that in the future its programs will not result in the displacement of more low-income people of color. The larger problem is that the city does no tracking of displacement at all, and thus cannot evaluate the disparate racial impacts of its policies and adjust its programs to reduce displacement.

Since the city no longer values permanent affordability, it is forever facing a crisis in affordable housing, always having to spend billions to catch up. Not coincidentally, since the 1980s and the end of funding for newly constructed public housing, the city has also been locked into a problem of chronic homelessness, with more people sleeping in shelters now than ever before. More shelters, a few new housing units created by inclusionary zoning, more subsidized housing that is not permanently affordable, and much more market-rate housing — these are not solutions but symptoms of a chronic housing problem.

## HABITAT VS. HOUSING

The United Nations Centre for Human Settlements considers the right to housing as much more than the right to a roof over one's head. The roof provides shelter, but shelter is not housing. The right to housing also includes a safe, healthy living environment. Though seemingly forgotten, the 1949 Housing Act passed by Congress proposed that housing be provided "in a decent living environment."

Yet there is another critical aspect to the right to housing. According to the United Nations Special Rapporteur on the Right to Adequate Housing, it includes security of tenure. In other words, the right to stay. Displacement, being forced to move, is a violation of a basic human right (De Schutter and Rolnik 2013).

Security of tenure has not been a driving force behind New York City's housing policies. The driving force has been the creation of shelter, not housing or the right to housing. The city's housing agency, the Department of Housing Preservation and Development (HPD), has become a de facto landlord for many low-income tenants in communities of color. However, since neither HPD nor DCP has a comprehensive strategy for dealing with the living environments where these housing units are located, HPD can at best be a benign absentee landlord, and at worst a slumlord. If it is going to provide decent housing, HPD must also make it a priority to engage with communities in a comprehensive way. HPD and DCP, and many other city agencies, are operating in their own silos. This is all the more reason for the city to value community-based planning for its ability to bridge the gaps within city government as well as within neighborhoods.

Housing in the public domain, whether under the jurisdiction of NYCHA or HPD, can be re-imagined as a critical community resource. The city can encourage the formation of community land trusts in which the local community retains control over the land, guaranteeing security of tenure, but with continuing support and involvement from city government.[2] The

**06.C Demonstration Opposing City's Rezonings, 2015.**

*Photo: Tom Angotti, 2015.*

housing agencies can and should be actively engaged in community-based planning and all issues that affect the built environment. Whatever form it takes, however, the critical change that needs to take place is for housing to be reconceived as habitat.

# WHERE WE GO FROM HERE

To sum up, here are some ideas about how the analysis and critique embodied in this book can be turned into new policies and real change. This is only an outline and a beginning. The most important step forward is to open up a broad public discussion and not allow these critical issues to be sidelined by pragmatic calls to make minor adjustments in policies and practices that are outmoded, discriminatory, and exacerbating gross inequalities in the city.

### Make Fundamental Changes in the Way of Thinking
- Acknowledge that race (still) matters at all levels of government
- Make planning a priority and zoning one of many by-products of planning
- Recognize community-based planning as an essential function of government
- Diversify the planning profession
- Develop habitat and not just housing
- Integrate agency agendas with communities, and not just programs, in mind
- Monitor and control residential and business displacement

## Slow Down and Take Time to Plan

- New York City must have a comprehensive long-term planning strategy that is widely discussed and debated and officially approved. The strategy should establish the context for community-based planning and confront the challenges of regional planning. PlaNYC 2030 was a beginning, but it was done in a very short period of time and involved a small group of professionals. It failed to seriously incorporate input from the city's diverse communities. The city's planning strategy must be subject to approval in accordance with Section 197-a of the city charter.
- Integrate all aspects of urban life in the planning process and do not limit planning to physical land use planning and zoning.
- Make racial and economic equality a fundamental objective for planning at all levels. This requires constant oversight and auditing by competent independent bodies. A diverse panel of advocates for racial justice drawn from the faculty of the City University of New York should be commissioned to provide this oversight.
- Reform the environmental review process so that the key issues of environmental and public health are part of the public discussion and debate about land use changes. Presently too many environmental reviews are only voluminous and highly technical reports prepared to meet legal requirements but the critical issues they deal with are rarely subject to open discussion.

## Institutionalize and Honor Community-Based Planning

- Give more power and resources to community boards
- Guarantee that every community board have a full-time planner trained not just in zoning but in the complex, integrated approaches to community-based planning
- Hold all community boards accountable to inclusionary and democratic principles
- Revise the rules for 197-a plans to facilitate more inclusive, integrated planning that respects environmental justice and fair share principles
- Incorporate firm legally binding proposals in 197-a plans, including items that must be incorporated in the operating and capital budgets
- Require approved 197-a plans as a prerequisite for a major rezoning; these plans need to be updated at least every five years.

## Put Zoning in its Place

- Require that major rezoning actions be consistent with a community-based plan and the city's strategic, comprehensive plan
- End the use of short-term planning exercises and "visioning" in communities that are tightly controlled by a small number of groups and individuals, especially when these exercises are used mainly to justify rezonings. It is important that all communities be challenged to "envision" a better future, but we need to rely on deep, democratic processes and not focus groups that come straight from Madison Avenue.
- Require that prior to every major rezoning there be a detailed study and analysis of displacement trends in the area, changes in land values and rents, and the effect of these trends on different economic, racial, and ethnic groups. The study should engage diverse residents and businesses. The results should be subject to extensive public scrutiny and discussion and not simply tucked away in environmental impact studies.

## Shift from Promoting "Affordable Housing" to Securing "Housing in the Public Domain"

- Guarantee that the city's housing programs provide housing for households earning between 40 and 80 percent of the local community median income, not the federally defined Area Median Income.
- In all new city-financed housing, give priority to homeless individuals and households.
- In all city housing programs, affordability should be guaranteed in perpetuity.
- The city, state, and federal governments should provide capital funds for the construction of new low-income housing and the maintenance of existing low-income housing instead of spending its scarce resources on subsidies to developers and instead of prioritizing only middle-income housing.
- Place all publicly subsidized housing in community land trusts that guarantee permanent affordability, community control, and continuing government support.
- Stop the creeping privatization of the New York City Housing Authority.

## Take Displacement and Its Racial Consequences Seriously

- Establish a funded citywide task force on displacement and race. The membership and staff of the task force should reflect the city's racial and ethnic diversity and establish strong links with community and tenant organizations and advocates. It should be responsible for collecting data through action research, surveys, and interviews, and make these widely available to the public.
- The task force would create a repository for data and research on displacement that is open and accessible to the public.
- The city should undertake a long-term study and analysis of displacement trends in the city and region, and the ways that displacement affects trends in racial segregation and the socioeconomic well-being of people who are displaced.
- The city must commit many more resources to implement strategies that prevent the displacement of low-income people and communities of color. While the city's recent funding of legal assistance to tenants in housing court may have helped, it is a stop-gap measure that is too little and too late. Serious reforms will require more lasting solutions that address the biases in city institutions that feed displacement and racial discrimination.
- Require that all community-based plans and major rezonings consider the potential long-term effects on the displacement of households — not simply as part of the required environmental review but as a separate, independent endeavor.
- Pass the Small Business Jobs Survival Act to protect small, locally owned businesses and cultural spaces from displacement due to rising rents and real estate speculation.
- Repeal the city's "mixed-use" zoning and undertake a serious effort to create neighborhoods in which jobs and housing are integrated and available to working people, especially low-income minority communities. As in the past, mixed-use communities can thrive if the city uses its tax and regulatory powers to keep the lid on land prices instead of stimulating their rise, as with its faux mixed-use zoning districts.
- Tighten zoning restrictions in industrial districts to stop the incursion of hotels and other uses that lead to increases in land prices and pressures that displace established businesses.

# FROM ZONING OUT TO ZONING IN ON RACIAL JUSTICE

We started this narrative by calling attention to the uprooting of people and entire communities in New York City. This process is the result of a medley of real estate speculation and official land use policy. In a city that projects an image of inclusion and diversity, the endemic segregation and incessant displacement of low-income people and communities of color point to a far more problematic reality than the one imbedded in the myth of the melting pot.

Race (still) matters. We are not living in a color-blind, post-racial city. Yet city policy does not recognize the disparate impact of its land use and housing policies as they stimulate and reinforce market forces that displace people who have the fewest options for alternative housing. The city does not even attempt to measure displacement. The city's planning agency abets displacement through its zoning powers. It fails to monitor and understand the displacement process and it does nothing about it. The city's affordable housing programs fail to reach the people that need housing the most, and instead of dealing with housing as one of many elements that make up a decent living environment narrowly focuses on the production of housing units—that is, shelter instead of housing. Instead of treating housing as a human right, the city plays a numbers game, adding up units without taking responsibility for the creation of a healthy environment and stable communities.

We have presented three examples of communities that were zoned out: Brooklyn's Williamsburg, Harlem, and Manhattan's Chinatown. We could have given many more examples. Now is the time to stop the zoning machine and insist on a more humane and just way of bringing about change in our communities. Now is the time to demand planning—not phony focus-group tactics but real in-depth planning—as a serious alternative to zoning. Now we need to unmask the affordable housing scams.

The city must recognize that planning can be employed to address racial disparities. However, New York City does not engage in long-term comprehensive planning, either at the neighborhood, citywide, or regional level. It uses zoning without planning. It is time to create a vibrant urban democracy by giving community boards the power and resources to plan for the future of their neighborhoods in close cooperation with residents, businesses, and community-based organizations. By itself this will not be enough. There must be a fundamental shift in the way of thinking about planning and community. Community boards and planners should reflect our city's diversity. They should be held accountable to principles of racial justice and socioeconomic equality. But this will not happen unless city officials themselves, at all levels of government, make racial equality an integral element in their principles and practices. For community-based planning to be equitable and just, there must also be citywide planning based on principles of equity and justice.

Then we may go from being zoned out to zoning in on racial injustice.

**06.D  A Rally from the 1970's Against Eviction and Displacement in Midtown Manhattan.**

*Photo: Tom Angotti.*

**Endnotes**
1. The American Planning Association is at www.planning.org and Planners Network is at www.plannersnetwork.org.

2. For information about community land trusts in New York City, see http://nyccli.org.

# REFERENCES

Acitelli, Tom
> 2016 "East New York's Transformation Has Started: Who is Benefiting?" *Crain's*. January 21.

Airoldi, Donna M.
> 2015 "Chinatown Residents Protest 'Slumlord' Owner of Their Buildings," *DNAInfo.com*, May 19. http://www.dnainfo.com/new-york/20150519/chinatown/chinatown-residents-protest-slumlord-owner-of-their-buildings

Amzallag, Daniel
> 2008 "VOTE Files Lawsuit Challenging 125th Street Rezoning," *Columbia Spectator*, April 28. http://columbiaspectator.com/2008/04/28/vote-files-lawsuit-challenging-125th-street-rezoning

Anderson, Lincoln, Albert Amateau and Laurie Mittlemann
> 2008 "Rhetoric on Rezoning Ramps Up as Public Review Continues." *The Villager*. 78: 11, August 13–19.

Angotti, Tom
> 2010 *Land Use and the New York City Charter*. Report to the New York City Charter Commission, August 10.

> 2008 *New York For Sale: Community Planning Confronts Global Real Estate*. Cambridge: MIT Press.

> 2008a "Is New York's Sustainability Plan Sustainable?" http://www.hunter.cuny.edu/ccpd/repository/files/is-nycs-sustainability-plan-sustainable.pdf

> 2008b "Lovely Plan, Lousy Process," *The New York 2030 Notebook*. New York: Institute for Urban Design.

> 2005a "Zoning Instead of Planning in Williamsburg and Greenpoint," *Gotham Gazette*, May 17. http://www.gothamgazette.com/index.php/development/2767-zoning-instead-of-planning-in-williamsburg-and-greenpoint

> 1997 "New York City's '197-a' Community Planning Experience: Power to the People or Less Work for Planners?" *Planning Practice & Research* 12:1, 59-67.

> 1993 *Metropolis 2000: Planning, Poverty and Politics*. New York: Routledge.

Angotti, Tom and Kate Ervin
> 2008 *Analysis of Draft Environmental Impact Statement (DEIS) East Village/Lower East Side Rezoning*. Hunter College Center for Community Planning and Development.

Angotti, Tom and Sylvia Morse
> 2014 *Keeping the Public in Public Housing*, Hunter College Center for Community Planning & Development. https://tomangotti.files.wordpress.com/2014/04/keepingthepublicin publichousing.pdf

ANHD (Association for Neighborhood Housing and Development)
> 2013 "How Is Affordable Housing Threatened In Your Neighborhood?" http://www.anhd.org/wp-content/uploads/2011/07/Revised-Chart-4.2.13-FINAL-1.pdf

Anuta, Joe
  2016 "City announces Greenpoint affordable-housing deal that saves taxpayer dollars,"
  *Crain's New York Business*, June 26. http://www.crainsnewyork.com/article/20150626/
  REAL_ESTATE/150629913/city-announces-greenpoint-affordable-housing-deal-that-
  saves-taxpayer-dollars

Arieff, Irwin
  2009 "Momentum in South Harlem," *The New York Times*, December 24. http://www.
  nytimes.com/2009/12/27/realestate/27harlem.html?adxnnl=1&adxnnlx=1431009570-
  DopWapZYilqdTS8ooFk8NQ&_r=0

AALDEF (Asian American Legal Defense and Education Fund)
  2013. *Chinatown Then and Now*. http://aaldef.org/Chinatown%20Then%20and%20
  Now%20AALDEF.pdf

Bailey, Nellie
  2008 "Harlem: Resisting Displacements," *Black Star News*, June 16. http://www.
  blackstarnews.com/ny-watch/others/harlem-resisting-displacements.html#sthash.
  Tpxl1lY0.pdf

Brown, Eliot
  2007 "Rezoning Plan May Transform Area of Harlem," *The New York Sun*, October
  15. http://www.nysun.com/new-york/rezoning-plan-may-transform-area-of-
  harlem/64548

Barbino, Al
  2011 "Chinatown residents protest against landlords, complaining of bad conditions,
  harassment," *New York Daily News*. May 9.

Bauman, John F.
  2000 "The Roots of Federal Housing Policy," In *From Tenements to the Taylor Homes: In
  Search of an Urban Housing Policy in Twentieth-Century America*, John F. Bauman, Roger
  Biles, and Kristin M. Szylvian, eds. University Park, PA: Pennsylvania State University Press.

Buettner, Russ
  2014 "They Kept a Lower East Side Lot Vacant for Decades." *The New York Times*.
  March 21.

Brash, Julian
  2011 *Bloomberg's New York: Class and Governance in the Luxury City*. Athens: University
  of Georgia Press.

Brooks, Richard R.W. and Carol M. Rose
  2013 *Saving the Neighborhood: Racially Restrictive Covenants, Law, and Social Norms*.
  Cumberland, RI: Harvard University Press, 2013.

CAAAV
  2008 Organizing Asian Communities, and the Urban Justice Center. *Converting
  Chinatown: A Snapshot of a Neighborhood Becoming Unaffordable and Unlivable*.
  December. http://caaav.org/publications/ConvertingChinatownReport.pdf

Calavita, Nico and Alan Mallach, Eds.
  2010 *Inclusionary Housing in International Perspective*. Cambridge: Lincoln Institute
  of Land Policy.

Cardwell, Diane
  2011 "Tower Has Its Own Lawn, but Neighbors Still Look for Their Open Space," *The
  New York Times*, November 7. http://www.nytimes.com/2011/11/08/nyregion/a-
  williamsburg-giant-with-his-own-lawn-moves-in.html

Caro, Robert
 1975 *The Power Broker: Robert Moses and the Fall of New York*. New York: Vintage.

Cheshire, Paul
 2007 *Segregated Neighbourhoods and Mixed Communities*. Joseph Rowntree Foundation.

Chou, Jerome and Manuel Miranda
 2011 "Public Notice 1: SPURA," *Open City*. February 22. http://openthecity.org/?p=1739

City of New York
 2015 *Next Generation NYCHA*. May.

 2007 *PlaNYC2030*. http://www.nyc.gov/html/planyc/downloads/pdf/publications/full_report_2007.pdf

 2005 *Greenpoint-Williamsburg Inclusionary Housing Program*, Department of City Planning, November.

Community Service Society
 2014 *Strenghthening New York City's Public Housing: Directions for Change*.

Cuomo, Mario
 1974 *Forest Hills Diary*. New York: Random House.

Dai, Serena
 2014 "Greenpoint Landing, Williamsburg Get City Funding to Build Affordable Units," *DNAInfo.com*, June 16.

Dagen Bloom, Nicholas
 2008 *Public Housing That Worked: New York in the Twentieth Century*. Philadelphia: University of Pennsylvania Press.

De Paolo, Philip
 2004 "Hundreds to Demonstrate at Williamsburg-Greenpoint Waterfront for Affordable Housing," *Press Release*, November 18, 2004.

De Schutter, Olivier and Raquel Rolnik
 2013 "The Social Function of Land and Security of Tenure," *Take Back the Land! The Social Function of Land and Housing, Resistances & Alternatives*. Paris: AITEC.

Dean, John P.
 1947 "Only Caucasian: A Study of Race Covenants," *Journal of Land & Public Utility Economics*, 23:4, November, 428-432.

Del Signore, John
 2008 "Tenants Sue Owner of Big Harlem Building Over Displacement Tactics," *Gothamist*, October 16.

Dulchin, Benjamin, Moses Gates, and Barika Williams
 2014 "How Much Housing Can Inclusionary Zoning Produce?" *ANHD Blogs*, April 10. http://www.anhd.org/?p=4876

Feltz, Renee
 2008 "Redlining: Why So Few Harlemites Own Property," *The Indypendent*, February 22. https://indypendent.org/2008/02/22/redlining-why-so-few-harlemites-own-property

Ferguson, Sarah
 2005 "NYC pols want a Williamsburg Gold Coast. Cool kids and neighborhood vets say no way," *The Village Voice*, April 3. http://www.villagevoice.com/news/0514,ferguson,62681,5.html

Fitch, Robert .
  1993 *The Assassination of New York*. New York: Routledge.

Flint, Anthony
  2009 *Wrestling with Moses: How Jane Jacobs Took on New York's Master Builder and Transformed the American City*. New York: Random House.

Florida, Richard
  2017 *The New Urban Crisis*, New York: Basic Books.

Furman Center for Real Estate and Urban Policy
  2014 *State of the City's Housing & Neighborhoods in 2014*.

  2013 *State of New York City's Housing and Neighborhoods in 2013*.

  2011 *State of New York City's Housing & Neighborhoods, 2011*.

  2010 *How Have Recent Rezonings Affected the City's Ability to Grow?* Policy Brief, March.

  2005 *State of New York City's Housing and Neighborhoods in 2005*.

Fujioka, Gen
  2011 "Transit Oriented Development and Communities of Color: A Field Report," *Progressive Planning*, Winter. http://www.plannersnetwork.org/2011/01/transit-oriented-development-and-communities-of-color-a-field-report

Fullilove, Mindy Thompson
  2016 *Root Shock: How Tearing Up City Neighborhoods Hurts America and What We Can Do About It*. New York: New Village Press.

Gans, Herbert
  1962 *The Urban Villagers*. New York: Free Press.

Gill, Jonathan
  2011 *Harlem: The Four Hundred Year History from Dutch Village to Capital of Black America*. New York: Grove Press.

Goffe, Leslie
  2014 "The Harlem Gentrification: From Black to White," *New African Magazine*. June 25.

Goldberg, Leo
  2015 *Game of Zones: Neighborhood Rezonings and Uneven Urban Growth in Bloomberg's New York City*. Massachusetts Institute of Technology, Department of Urban Studies and Planning, Master's Thesis.

Gørrild, Marie, Sharon Obialo, and Nienke Venema
  2008 "Gentrification and Displacement in Harlem: How the Harlem Community Lost Its Voice en Route to Progress," *Humanity in Action*. http://www.humanityinaction.org/knowledgebase/79-gentrification-and-displacement-in-harlem-how-the-harlem-community-lost-its-voice-en-route-to-progress

Gregor, Alison
  2014 "Brooklyn: New Towers for Williamsburg," *The New York Times,* December 19. http://www.nytimes.com/2014/12/21/realestate/brooklyn-new-towers-for-williamsburg.html

Gregory, Kia
  2012 " A Boulevard in Harlem Undergoes a Resurgence," *The New York Times,* December 2. http://www.nytimes.com/2012/12/03/nyregion/a-harlem-resurgence-along-frederick-douglass-blvd.html?partner=rss&emc=rss

Hamm, Theodore
  2005 "Save Our City," *Brooklyn Rail*. May 1. http://www.brooklynrail.org/2005/05/local/save-our-city

**156**

Hartman, Chester, Dennis Keating, and Richard LeGates, with Steve Turner
  1981 *Displacement: How To Fight It*. San Francisco: Legal Services Anti-
  Displacement Project.

Heilpern, John
  2010 "Princess of the City," *Vanity Fair*. April 30.

Hoffman, Meredith
  2013 "City Built Less Than 2 Percent of Affordable Units Promised to Williamsburg,"
  *DNAInfo.com*, May 20. http://www.dnainfo.com/new-york/20130520/williamsburg/city-
  built-less-than-2-percent-of-affordable-units-promised-williamsburg

Hyra, Derek S.
  2008 *The New Urban Renewal: The Economic Transformation of Harlem and Bronzeville*.
  Chicago: University of Chicago Press.

Jackson, Kenneth
  2008 *Crabgrass Frontier: The Suburbanization of the United States*. New York: Oxford
  University Press.

Johnson, William A., Jr.
  2001 "Rochester: The Path Less Travelled" *Planners Network*. 148, July/August, 1, 14-15.

Keller, Emily
  2005 "Pols Gush, Nabes Grumble Over Rezoning," *Greenpoint Star*, May 5.

Keshner, Andrew
  2009 "Tenants, Landlord Square Off in West Harlem Affordable Housing Fight,"
  *The Uptowner*. December 15.

Khawaja, Ali
  2010 "Lower Manhattan Expressway." Research Paper, Harvard Graduate School of
  Design. www.gsd.harvard.edu/research/research_centers/zofnass/pdf/Lower%20
  Manhattan%20Expressway.pdf

Kwong, Peter
  1996 *The New Chinatown*. New York: Hill and Wang.

Kwong, Peter and Samuel Stein
  2015 "Preserve and Protect Chinatown." Roosevelt House Public Policy Institute at
  Hunter College, 2015. http://www.roosevelthouse.hunter.cuny.edu/devdev/wp-
  content/uploads/2015/02/Kwong_Stein_Issue_Brief-Chinatown2-5-15.pdf?f43020

Lee, Jennifer
  2009 "Harassment Is Focus of Chinatown Tenants' Suit," *The New York Times*,
  February 18.

Lees, Loretta, Tom Slater and Elvin Wyly
  2008 *Gentrification*. New York: Routledge.

Li, Bethany Y
  2010 "Zoned Out: Chinatown and Lower East Side Residents and Business Owners Fight
  to Stay in New York City," *Asian American Policy Review*. 19, 91-97.

Lin, Jan
  1998 *Reconstructing Chinatown: Ethnic Enclave, Global Change*. Minneapolis: University
  of Minnesota Press.

Little, Rivka Gewirtz
  2002 "The New Harlem: Who's Behind the Real Estate Gold Rush and Who's Fighting It?"
  *The Village Voice*. September 17.

Litvak, Ed
    2015 "Dept. of City Planning Rejects Expansive Chinatown Rezoning Proposal,"
    *The Lo-Down*. March 16.

    2014 "Extell Reveals Plans For 205-Unit Affordable Tower on Former Pathmark Site."
    *The Lo-Down*, June 12.

Madar, Josiah
    2016 "White Paper: Inclusionary Housing Policy in New York City: Assessing New
    Opportunities, Constraints, and Trade-offs," NYU Furman Center, March 26. http://
    furmancenter.org/files/NYUFurmanCenter_InclusionaryZoningNYC_March2015.pdf

Marcuse, Peter
    2014 "A Just Code of Ethics for Planners," *Progressive Planning*. 198, Winter. 16-19.

    1986 "Housing Policy and the Myth of the Benevolent State," *Critical Perspectives in
    Housing*. Rachel G. Bratt, Chester Hartman, and Ann Meyerson, eds. Philadelphia:
    Temple University Press, 248-263.

    1971 "Social Indicators and Housing Policy," *Urban Affairs Review Quarterly*, 7:2,
    December, 183-217.

Martinez, Miranda J.
    2010 *Power at the Roots: Gentrification, Community Gardens and the Puerto Ricans of the
    Lower East Side*. Lanham (MD): Lexington Books.

Massey, Douglas S. and Nancy A. Denton
    1993 *American Apartheid: Segregation and the Making of the Underclass*. Cambridge:
    Harvard University Press.

Maurrasse, David
    2006 *Listening to Harlem: Gentrification, Community, and Business*. New York:
    Taylor & Francis.

Meyer, Stephen Grant
    2001 *As Long As They Don't Move Next Door: Segregation And Racial Conflict In American
    Neighborhoods*. Lanham, Maryland: Rowman & Littlefield.

Morgenson, Gretchen
    2008 "Questions of Rent Tactics by Private Equity," *The New York Times*, May 9.

Moss, Jeremiah
    2015 "What is Authentically Harlem?" *Vanishing New York*. February 26 http://
    vanishingnewyork.blogspot.com/2015/02/what-is-authentically-harlem.html

Moynihan, Colin
    2007 "Columbia Announces Deal on Its 17-Acre Expansion Plan," *The New
    York Times*, September 27. http://a030-lucats.nyc.gov/lucats/ULURPRecord.
    aspx?ULURPonly=070495

Mohl, Raymond A.
    2000 "Planned Destruction: The Interstates and Central City Housing," in *From
    Tenements to the Taylor Homes: In Search of an Urban Housing Policy in Twentieth-
    Century America*. John F. Bauman, Roger Biles, and Kristin M. Szylvian, Eds. University
    Park, PA: Penn State University Press.

Mollenkopf, John H. and Manuel Castells, eds.
    1992 *Dual City: Restructuring New York*. New York: Russell Sage Foundation.

Municipal Art Society
    n.d. *The Will to Plan: Community-Initiated Planning in New York City*. New York.

    1998 *The State of 197-a Planning in New York City*. New York.

Nahmias, Laura
2015 "De Blasio defends market rate housing on NYCHA land." *Politico New York*, August 24.

Navarro, Mireya
2015 "Public Housing Residents Wary of Mayor de Blasio's Plan." *The New York Times*, May 19.

Newman, Kathe, et. al,
2007 *Gentrification and Rezoning: Williamsburg-Greenpoint, Community Development Studio*, Rutgers University, Spring. http://rwv.rutgers.edu/wp-content/uploads/2013/08/2007_SPRING_CD_Studio_Presentation_Text.pdf

Pasquarelli, Adrianne
2015 "Hotels in trendy nabes hem in manufacturers," *Crain's New York Business*, March 8. http://www.crainsnewyork.com/article/20150308/HOSPITALITY_TOURISM/150309872/hotels-in-trendy-nabes-hem-in-manufacturers

Pietila, Antero
2010 *Not in My Neighborhood: How Bigotry Shaped a Great American City*. Chicago: Ivan R. Dee.

Pinto, Nick
2015 "'It's A Land Grab: NYCHA Tenants Protest Private Development Plans For Public Land." *Gothamist*, October 21. http://gothamist.com/2015/10/21/nycha_deblasio_protest.php

Plitt, Amy
2015 "Greenpoint Landing's Affordable Rentals Will Ask From $494,"*Curbed NY*, December 3. http://ny.curbed.com/archives/2015/1/03/greenpoint_landings_affordable_rentals_will_ask_from_494.php

Pratt Center for Community Development and the Collective for Community, Culture and the Environment
2013 *Chinatown Planning and Rezoning Study, Draft Task 2 Report: Research and Analysis*. http://www.chinatownworkinggroup.org/2013-07-11%20Planner%20Research%20(Draft).pdf

Rabin, Yale
1989 "Expulsive Zoning: The Inequitable Legacy of Euclid," in *Zoning and the American Dream: Promises Still to Keep*, Charles M. Haar and Jerold S. Kayden, eds. Chicago: APA Planners Press.

*Report of the National Advisory Commission on Civil Disorders*.
1968 New York: Bantam.

Rich, Motoko
2003 "For Harlem Homebuyers, Prices Head North, *The New York Times*, November 20. http://www.nytimes.com/2003/11/20/garden/for-harlem-homebuyers-prices-head-north.html

Rinn, Natalie
2013 "Greenpointers Protest 'Homogenized, Pasteurized, Sanitized, Supersized' Waterfront Development," *Bedford and Bowery*, August 14. http://bedfordandbowery.com/2013/08/greenpointers-protest-homogenized-pasteurized-sanitized-supersized-waterfront-development

Roberts, Sam
2014 "Manhattan's Income Gap is Widest in U.S., Census Finds," *The New York Times*, September 8.

2010 "No Longer Majority Black, Harlem Is in Transition," *The New York Times*, January 5.

Rosenberg, Eli
2014 "How NYC's Decade of Rezoning Changed the City of Industry," *Curbed*, January 16. http://ny.curbed.com/archives/2014/01/16/how_nycs_decade_of_rezoning_changed_the_city_of_industry.php

Rosenzweig, Roy and Betsy Blackmar
1994 *A History of Central Park: The Park and the People*. New York: Holt.

Rothstein, Richard
2017 *The Color of Law*. New York: Liveright

Sites, William
2003 *Remaking New York: Primitive Globalization and the Politics of Urban Community*. Minneapolis: University of Minnesota Press.

Slatin, Peter
2012 "Rezoning Transforms Character of Harlem Boulevard," *The New York Times*, March 27.

Smith, Greg B.
2015 "EXCLUSIVE: NYCHA Quietly Selling Off Parking Lots, Green Space, Playgrounds to Help Ease Budget Woes," *New York Daily News*. March 29.

2013 "High and Mighty NYCHA: Luxury Towers on Leased Land Would 'Look Down' on Projects," *New York Daily News*. June 11.

Smith, Neil and Peter Williams, eds.
1986 *Gentrification of the City*. Boston: Allen & Unwin.

Stringer, Scott M.
2014 *The Growing Gap: New York City's Housing Affordability Challenge*. Office of the New York City Comptroller, April.

Strozier, Matthew
2015 "For Harlem corridor, project on every block," *The Real Deal*, June 1. http://therealdeal.com/issues_articles/for-harlem-corridor-project-on-every-block

Susser, Ida and Filip A. Stabrowski,
2015 "Unaffordable Housing: A Case Study," Roosevelt House, Hunter College, February. http://www.roosevelthouse.hunter.cuny.edu/devdev/wp-content/uploads/2015/02/Susser_Stabrowski_2-10-151.pdf?b94997

Taylor, Dorceta E.
2014 *Toxic Communities: Environmental Racism, Industrial Pollution, and Residential Mobility*. New York: NYU Press.

Thabit, Walter
2003 *How East New York Became a Ghetto*. New York: NYU Press.

Toy, Vivian S.
2006 "Luxury Condos Arrive in Chinatown," *The New York Times,* September 17.

Trotta, Daniel
2006 "Black New York Frets the Changing Face of Harlem," *Reuters*, August 18. redorbit.com/news/general/622349/black_new_york_frets_the_changing_face_of_harlem/index.html

Tucker, Maria Luisa
2008 "Lower East Side Rezone Sparks Border War in Chinatown," *Village Voice*, May 20.

Turner, Joan
1984 "Building Boundaries: The Politics of Urban Renewal in Manhattan's Lower East Side." PhD Dissertation, City University of New York.

Umbach, Greg (Fritz) and Dan Wishnoff
    2008 "Strategic Self-Orientalism: Urban Planning Policies and the Shaping of New York City's Chinatown, 1950–2005," *Journal of Planning History*, 7, 214–238.

Weiman, Vanessa
    2007 "Chinatown: Cracking the Fortune Cookie." *The Real Deal.* October 24.

Williams, Timothy
    2006 "Land Dispute Pits Columbia Vs. Residents In West Harlem," *The New York Times.* November 20.

    2008 "Mixed Feelings as Change Overtakes 125th St.," *The New York Times*, June 13.

Wright, Gwendolyn
    1981 *A Social History of Housing in America*. Cambridge: MIT Press.

Xu, Nannan
    2013 *Why Chinatown Has Gentrified Later Than Other Communities in Downtown Manhattan: A Planning History*. Master's Thesis in Urban Planning, Columbia University. http://academiccommons.columbia.edu/item/ac:162153

# CONTRIBUTOR BIOS

**TOM ANGOTTI** is Professor Emeritus of Urban Policy and Planning at Hunter College, the Graduate Center, and City University of New York, and directed the Hunter College Center for Community Planning & Development. He is adjunct professor at Parsons/The New School and the author of *New York for Sale: Community Planning Confronts Global Real Estate*, which won the 2009 Davidoff Book Award.

**PHILIP DePAOLO** is a long-time community activist who has been fighting issues of gentrification and poor zoning policies throughout New York City. He was formerly a resident of Williamsburg, Brooklyn.

**PETER MARCUSE** was Professor Emeritus, Department of Urban Planning at the Columbia University Graduate School of Architecture, Planning and Preservation. He (1928–2022) wrote extensively on urban planning and housing.

**SYLVIA MORSE** is a lifelong New Yorker who has dedicated her work to advancing community planning, the solidarity economy, and housing justice. She has worked with New York City nonprofits, city agencies, and grassroots organizations on local land use struggles, development of worker-owned cooperative businesses, and a range of housing programs and policy issues. She has a master's degree in urban planning from CUNY Hunter College.

**SAMUEL STEIN** is a geographer, urban planner and housing policy analyst living and working in New York City. He is the author of *Capital City* and his writing on planning politics has been published by *Jacobin, The Journal of Urban Affairs, The Guardian*, and many other magazines, newspapers and journals.